Patents, Trademarks and Copyrights

Practical Strategies for Protecting Your Ideas and Inventions

Second Edition

By
David G. Rosenbaum

Patents, Trademarks and Copyrights

Practical Strategies for Protecting Your Ideas and Inventions

Second Edition

By
David G. Rosenbaum

CAREER PRESS
180 Fifth Avenue
P.O. Box 34
Hawthorne, NJ 07507
1-800-CAREER-1
201-427-0229 (outside U.S.)
FAX: 201-427-2037

PATENTS, TRADEMARKS AND COPYRIGHTS: PRACTICAL STRATEGIES FOR PROTECTING YOUR IDEAS AND INVENTIONS
ISBN 1-56414-085-7, $8.95
Cover design by The Gottry Communications Group, Inc.
Series Editor: Richard L. Strohm
Produced by Ronald Adamson, Tucson
Printed in the U.S.A. by Book-mart Press

To order this title by mail, please include price as noted above, $2.50 handling per order, and $1.00 for each book ordered. Send to: Career Press, Inc., 180 Fifth Ave., P.O. Box 34, Hawthorne, NJ 07507.

Or call toll-free 1-800-CAREER-1 (Canada: 201-427-0229) to order using VISA or MasterCard, or for further information on books from Career Press.

Library of Congress Cataloging-in-Publication Data

Rosenbaum, David G., 1956-
    Patents, trademarks, and copyrights : practical strategies for protecting your ideas and inventions / by David G. Rosenbaum.--2nd ed.
        p. cm.
    Includes index.
    ISBN 1-56414-085-7 : $8.95
    1. Patent laws and legislation--United States--Popular works. 2. Trademarks--United States--Popular works. 3. Copyright--United States--Popular works. I. Title.
KF2980.R67 1994
346.7304'8--dc20
[347.30648]
                                                                        94-2173
                                                                        CIP

DEDICATION

· ·

For Susan, Stephanie, Matthew and Mara who are my foundation; together we explore the daily wonders of life. For Mom and Dad who always challenged me to be inquisitive, explorative, creative and open-minded.

A special thanks to Tricia Deutsch, a wonderful lady who makes it easy to come to work each day.

My profound gratitude to each and every one of my clients. You are the creative minds who constantly think of new and exciting ideas and inventions which challenge me to continue learning. Thank you.

To everyone who has the courage to create, I hope that this book will be only the first step to a most satisfying set of experiences.

TABLE OF CONTENTS

Introduction   1

Chapter One
Intellectual Property: What's That?   4

Chapter Two
Patents   9
    What is a Patent?   9
    What is Patentable?   9
    How Do I Get a Patent?   10
        Patent Searching   13
        Is the Idea Novel and Non-Obvious?   16
    Applying for a Patent   20
        Filing the Application with the U.S. Patent
            and Trademark Office   23
        Patent Office Examination of the Application   24
    What Protection Does My Patent Provide? 26

Chapter Three
Trademarks and Service Marks   30
    What is a Trademark?   30
    How Do I Get a Trademark?   31
    How Do I Register the Trademark?   33
    How Do I Keep My Trademark?   41

Chapter Four
Copyrights   42
    What is a Copyright?   43
    How Do I Get a Copyright?   44
    What is Copyrightable?   45
    How Do I Get a Copyright?   46
    How Long Does a Copyright Last?   49

Do I Need to Register the Copyright?   50
How Do I Register a Copyright?   51
How Do I Enforce My Copyright?   55

Chapter Five
Trade Secrets   56

Appendix A   59
Appendix B   75
Appendix C   79
Appendix D   83
Appendix E   88
Appendix F   90
Appendix G   91
Appendix H   92
Appendix I   93
Appendix J   94
Appendix K   95
Appendix L   97
Appendix M   98
Appendix N   100
Appendix O   102
Appendix P   103
Appendix Q   104
Appendix R   106

INTRODUCTION

We have all purchased articles which bear cryptic markings referring to patents, trademarks or copyrights. Hardly a day passes without most of us encountering products marked with symbols such as ™, ℠, ®, ©, Pat. No., or Patent Pending. While we are familiar with these markings, most people do not know what they mean, why they are put on products, or how these symbols convey legal rights in the products. The laws of Patents, Trademarks and Copyrights, generally referred to as Intellectual Property Law, each protect distinct ownership rights to different aspects of the product.

Patent rights and copyrights are unique. They are the only property rights which were provided for by the United States Constitution. Article 1, section 8, clause 8 of the Constitution provides that "Congress shall have the power ... [t]o promote the progress of science and useful arts, by securing for limited times to authors and inventors the exclusive right too their respective writings and discoveries."

Winning or losing on business opportunities may depend upon whether your ideas are protected by patents, trademarks or copyrights.

Winning or losing out on business and financial opportunities may depend upon whether your ideas, inventions, products and business are protected by patents, trademarks or copyrights. Ideas, inventions, products and business services are the basis of many highly successful businesses. Successful business owners and entrepreneurs typically place a high value on such "Intellectual Property."

Businesses have been won or lost because of their owners' efforts to protect their intellectual property or their failure to protect it by patents, trademarks or copyrights. The value of publicly traded stock has taken huge swings based principally upon whether the company has been successful in obtaining or enforcing its patent rights. There are many common myths and misunderstandings surrounding the need for and the difficulty in obtaining patent, trademark or copyright protection. Understanding the protection process and appreciating the valuable rights which can be acquired ensures that your intellectual property is protected.

Understanding the protection process ensures that your intellectual property is protected.

The book explains what protection is provided by patents, trademarks and copyrights, de-mystifies the process of obtaining patents, registered trademarks and copyrights and offers a guide to planning for and using patents, trademarks and copyrights. The book answers common questions such as:

- Do I need a patent, trademark or copyright?

- How do I obtain a patent, trademark of copyright?

- How can I protect the idea or invention concept before filing for a patent?

- Can I get a patent, trademark or copyright?

- What does the U.S. Patent and Trademark Office or the Copyright Office do and what should I expect to happen?

- How much does it cost to get my patent, trademark of copyright?

- What can I do with my patent, trademark or copyright now that I have it?

The answers to these questions will undoubtedly lead to many other questions. This area of the law can be very complicated, but can also lead to tremendous protection for your ideas. You are encouraged to take the time to ask your questions and make sure you understand the answers.

CHAPTER ONE
INTELLECTUAL PROPERTY:
WHAT'S THAT?

The term "intellectual property" generically describes a field of law which relates to rights in intangible property which is created by someone's intellectual effort. Fundamentally, rights in intangible property are virtually identical to rights in tangible property. The difference is that you can see and touch tangible property while intangible property must be described or depicted in some tangible form. Tangible property includes land, motor vehicles, houses, bicycles, jewelry, all of which can be held and physically possessed. On the other hand, you cannot see and physically possess intellectual property rights, but they can still exist if you take the time to understand what they are and how they can be protected.

> *You cannot see and physically possess intellectual property rights, but they can still exist.*

The concepts of patent, copyright, registration for trademarks and service marks and trade secret are all legal devices. These devices have been developed to document intellectual property rights and allow someone to own, control and transfer ownership in the intellectual property. Each device was developed to cover specific types of intellectual property. For example, patents protect machines, manufacturing processes and chemical formulations; copyrights cover music, lyrics, books, computer programs and pictures; trademarks and service marks cover names and logos used in connection with the marketing and sales of products and services; and trade secrets cover many different types of information which is valuable to its owner and is not generally available to competitors. The nature of the idea determines whether it is best protected by a patent, a copyright, a trademark or service mark or a trade secret.

Of the different types of protection for intellectual property, only patents require approval of a government agency to acquire and own. With certain important exceptions, copyrights, trademarks, service marks and trade secrets are created and owned by the person or company creating or developing them. This is the case irrespective of whether or not any filing or registration is made with either a state or federal agency.

The nature of the idea determines whether it is best protected by a patent, a copyright, a trademark or a trade secret.

Patents are a matter of exclusive federal statutory law. In foreign countries, the foreign country's national government regulates issuance of patents in those countries. The United States statutes found at Title 35 of the United States Code define the types of things a patent can cover, the conditions and requirements for patentability, the rights granted by an award of a patent and the rights of a patent owner to enforce those patent rights.

Trademarks and service marks are governed both by federal statutory law and state law in all fifty states. Names, logo designs, packaging design, architectural design, interior design, package or product design and slogans may all be protected merely by using them and having your customers come to associate that identity with your product or service. Using a trademark, service mark, trade name or trade dress for a product or service establishes so called "common law" rights in the market area in which the use occurs. Market area may be geographical or may be the area in which your products are distributed or your services are advertised or provided.

In addition to common law rights, all states and the federal government provide a system for registering trademarks and service marks. Both the state and federal registration systems require that you file an application with the appropriate administering agency office, have the application reviewed by the agency office, and, if approved, the registration will issue. Upon issuance of a registration, your rights are determined by the state or federal statutes under which the registration was granted and issued. These registration rights supplement, not supersede, your common law rights.

Under the federal registration system, you are permitted to apply for a registration prior to actually using the trademark or service mark or upon actual use of the mark. An application filed before use of the mark must, however, be based upon a genuine or "*bona fide*" intention to use the trademark or service mark. This type of application is termed an "Intent to Use" registration application. An application based upon a prior actual use is termed an "Actual Use" registration application. The principal difference between the two types of applications is that an Intent to Use application, once approved, does not mature into a registered mark until you have made actual commercial use of the mark. An Actual Use application, once approved, will mature into a registered mark because it is based upon continuous previous commercial use of the mark on or in connection with a product or service. The federal laws relating to trademark and service mark protection and enforcement are found in Title 15 of the United States Code.

Copyrights, like patents, are controlled exclusively by federal law. Title 17 of the United States Code covers the law of copyright. Copyright is a form of protection granted to authors of "original works of authorship" including literary, dramatic, musical, artistic and other types of intellectual work, such a computer programs. Unlike patents, copyright protection exists immediately at the time the author creates the work in a "fixed" or tangible form. The mere act of putting the work in a fixed or tangible form gives rise to the copyright and the copyright immediately becomes the property of the author who created the work. Only an author or co-author, or those who derive rights through the author, can claim copyright to a given work.

Unlike patents, copyright protection exists immediately at the time the author creates the work in tangible form.

Copyrights can exist for textual works, works of visual art, works of performing art, sound recordings, serial works and mask works. Textual works include, for example, song lyrics, books, poems, movie or theatrical scripts. Works of visual art include paintings, sculpture, photographs, illustrations or holograms. Works of performing art include, for example, dance choreography, theatrical performances, video taped recordings of speeches or even a video tape of a motion picture. Sound recordings may include music recorded on a compact disc, a phonograph record, a cassette, or possibly multi-media computer readable recordings on compact discs known as CD-ROMs. Serial works include any type of regularly published magazine, such as Time or Newsweek, a daily or weekly newspaper, or even a monthly business report. Lastly, mask works are a specialized type of image used as templates in the manufacture of integrated circuits or other microelectronic equipment.

Finally, trade secrets can be virtually any information, maintained confidential by its owner, which gives its owner a commercial advantage over competitors. Perhaps the best known trade secret is the formula for Coca-Cola which has remained a highly valuable trade secret for well over one hundred years. Trade secrets exist under state law and enforcement is under either a common law or statutory system in each state. Many states have adopted a version of a Uniform Trade Secrets Act seeking to make trade secrets law more uniform among all the states.

Now that you have an idea about the different types of protection available, it is necessary to look into each type of protection in greater detail.

Perhaps the best known trade secret is the formula for Coca-Cola.

CHAPTER TWO
PATENTS
. . . .

What is a Patent?

A patent gives to an inventor the right to exclude all others from making, using, or selling the invention within the United States and its territories. Owning a patent **does not** give you the exclusive right to make, use or sell the invention. Like other legal rights, patent rights must be enforced by making a claim that someone is making, using or selling the invention without your permission. Title 35 United States Code (35 U.S.C.) Section 154 provides "Every patent shall . . . grant to the patentee . . . the right to exclude others from making, using, or selling the invention throughout the United States."

Like other legal rights, patent rights must be enforced by making a claim.

There are three types of patents. First, utility patents are granted to the inventor of a new and useful process, machine, manufacture, composition of matter, or any new and useful improvement. Examples include, a new process for filtering drinking water, a new machine or device for filtering drinking water, a new method for making the water filter or even the filter material itself. You may hear some people refer to "use patents," "device patents," or "process patents." Each of these terms describe what the patent covers or claims rather than a patent type; all describe utility patents. An example of a utility patent for a water filter is found at Appendix A. Second, design patents are issued for new, original and ornamental designs for manufactured articles. For example, a design patent may be granted for the design of an automobile body, or for the design of a piece of furniture. An example of a design patent is provided at Appendix B. This patent covers a design for the water filter described and covered by the utility patent found at Appendix A. Third, plant patents are granted for distinct and new varieties of asexually reproduced plants, such as patented roses or chrysanthemums.

The term of a utility patent is seventeen years from date of issuance by the United States Patent and Trademark Office. The term of a design patent is fourteen years. The term of a plant patent is seventeen years.

While not a separate and distinct type of patent, re-issue patents exist. Re-issue patents do not extend or renew the life of the original patent. Rather, the patent laws provide for reissuance of a patent to correct errors made without deceptive intent in the originally issued patent, which cause the originally issued patent to be wholly or partly inoperative or invalid. The term of a reissue patent is for the balance of the original seventeen year term.

What is Patentable?

Subject matter which is patentable is defined at 35 U.S.C. §101 as any "process, machine, manufacture or composition of matter" or any "improvement thereof."

Examples of patentable subject matter include the following:

A process may involve treating a material to produce a particular result or product, or may involve manipulating tangible matter to produce a desired end result. Examples: tempering glass to make it break-resistant or transferring genes encoding a protein from a bacterium to a plant or animal to induce expression of the protein in the plant or animal. Processes can also refer to a new use for a known composition or apparatus, e.g., a pharmaceutical or a machine. Example: using a known asthma drug to suppress pre-term labor contractions. Process patents protect manipulative steps combined to produce an end result, i.e., mixing, heating, cooling, crystallizing, etc.

Tempering glass to make it break resistant is an example of a patentable process.

A *machine* is a device which performs a useful operation, usually having mechanical or electrical elements, such as, for example, springs, hinges, transistors, or resistors.

A *composition* of matter is a combination of two or more substances, and can include chemical elements or compositions, such as a soft drink formulation or a drug.

A *manufacture* is a catch-all category for the remaining statutory subject matter which is not a process, machine or composition. A manufacture may be a man-made genetically engineered bacterium which is capable of breaking down crude oil.

Certain types of things cannot be patented because they are non-patentable subject matter:

- methods of doing business

- mental processes

- mathematical algorithms

- naturally occurring articles

- scientific principles

Once it is determined that an idea relates to something which is patentable subject matter, three additional requirements must be met before the idea can be considered patentable.

First, the idea must relate to something which is useful. Usually, this requirement is met virtually without any thought given to it. However, it is a critical element and cannot be overlooked. Always ask yourself the question, "What is my idea useful for and why?" Once you have convinced yourself of its utility, you should have no trouble convincing the U.S. Patent and Trademark Office if it becomes an issue.

Always ask yourself the question, "What is my idea useful for and why?"

Second, the idea must be novel. This novelty requirement means that the subject matter is "new." Essentially, the novelty requirement is met if the subject matter has not previously been publicly known or used by others, or was not the subject of a prior patent or printed publication published more than one year from the invention of the subject matter.

Third, the idea must not be obvious to one having ordinary skill in the relevant technical discipline to which the invention relates. The non-obviousness requirement is found at 35 U.S.C. §103, and provides that a patent shall not be granted if, at the time the invention was made, the "differences between the subject matter sought to be patented and the prior art are such that the subject matter as a whole would have been obvious ... to a person having ordinary skill in the art to which the subject matter pertains...". The non-obviousness requirement is a subjectively-applied objective test, which requires an analysis of the scope and content of the prior art and a determination of the level of "ordinary skill" in the field of art.

How Do I Get a Patent?

Only inventors, attorneys or agents admitted to practice before the U.S. PTO can file and prosecute patent applications. The Patent and Trademark Office strongly recommends that you both consult with and retain a patent attorney or agent to represent you in your dealings with the Patent and Trademark Office. While you are allowed to file and prosecute your own patent application, you **must** follow all Rules of Practice and Ethics before the PTO which are found at Title 37 Code of Federal Regulations. In addition to the Rules of Practice and Ethics, the Patent and Trademark Office has numerous practices and procedures which are peculiar to obtaining a patent.

The Patent and Trademark Office strongly recommends that you retain a patent attorney to represent you.

Patent Searching

Once you have determined that your idea relates to patentable subject matter, the next step is to determine whether your idea meets with the remaining conditions of patentability. Simply, you should evaluate your idea for utility, novelty and non-obviousness.

This patentability evaluation is usually termed "patent searching." Patent searching is almost always advisable. Patent searching can be done at the public search rooms of the U.S. Patent and Trademark Office in Arlington, Virginia. Searching may also be done at a Patent Depository Library, consisting of microfilm patents, located at Patent and Trademark Depository Libraries across the country. You will find the reference librarians at these Depository Libraries extremely helpful. A list of Patent and Trademark Depository Libraries is provided at Appendix C. There are many professional patent searchers, principally located either in Washington, D.C. or in Arlington, Virginia who can conduct a patent search for you. The patent searcher will provide you with copies of patents relevant to your idea, but usually do not provide any evaluation of the patents, nor do they usually provide a legal patentability opinion. Patent attorneys and patent agents also can perform a patent search. However, most patent attorneys and agents typically hire a professional patent searcher to conduct the actual search and the attorney or agent then reviews the search results and provides you with a legal patentability opinion.

Typically, the cost of hiring a patent searcher ranges from $75 to $350.

Typically, the cost of hiring a patent searcher ranges from $75 to $350. The typical cost of hiring a patent attorney or agent to conduct a patent search and render a patentability opinion ranges from $400 to $1,000. These costs vary depending upon the technical complexity of the idea and the thoroughness of the patent search.

If you choose to conduct your own patent search, you should expect to spend many, many hours both preparing for and conducting the search and many more hours reviewing the search results. In addition to the time, you will need to make photocopies of the patents you find, so take plenty of change with you.

Before going to the patents at either the U.S. Patent and Trademark Office or to a Depository Library, you will need to review a publication titled "Index of Patent Classification." All patents are classified, according to subject matter, by classes and subclasses. There are over 400 classes and over 20,000 sub-classes which cover literally every type of invention known to mankind. Think of the Index of Patent Classification as your Table of Contents to the patents. You will need to determine which classes and subclasses your idea relates to, look at the patents in those classes and subclasses, and determine which patents most closely relate to your idea. Once you have found a group of patents closely relating to your idea, you have established the scope and content of the "prior art" as represented by the issued United States Patents.

There are over 400 classes of patents which cover every type of invention known to mankind.

A search of the United States Patents **does not** constitute a complete patentability search. Patentability of your idea depends upon its novelty and non-obviousness in view of all publicly available or generally known information relating to your idea. You should keep in mind that United States Patents are only one source of such information. Other sources of information are foreign patents and published patent applications, scientific journals, technical bulletins, product literature and brochures, trade publications, press releases, and product or service catalogs. Patents and patent applications are generally termed "patent references," while non-patent literature is generally termed "non-patent references." While it would be desirable to evaluate patentability with reference to all relevant prior art, it is a monumental task to amass such a large and broad-ranging body of information. For this reason, patent searching generally looks only to United States Patents, relevant scientific or technical literature, and, if possible, foreign patents and published patent applications. These sources offer a good cross-section of the prior art and are readily available at reasonable cost.

Now for the hard part. After selecting the patents which most closely relate to your idea, you must decide whether your idea is novel and non-obvious in view of the prior art as represented by the patent and non-patent references uncovered by the search.

Is the Idea Novel and Non-Obvious?

Generally, your idea is novel if there is no single patent which discloses a similar device, process or design having all of the same elements arranged, ordered or assembled in the same manner as in your idea. This does not mean that the patent must be identical to your idea, only that it contain each and every element of your idea arranged in the same manner as your idea. For example:

Let's assume you have an idea for a widget made of parts A, B, C and D. If a single prior art reference discloses a widget having each of parts A, B, C and D, then your idea cannot be considered novel; it is simply not new. It does not matter if the widget also contains other elements in addition to A, B, C and D. However, if a single prior art reference discloses a widget which is made of A, B, C and E, element D is missing and your idea can be considered novel.

Once you have satisfied yourself that your idea is novel, you must determine whether your idea is non-obvious. Non-obviousness is one of the most difficult concepts of patent law. Your idea can be considered obvious if it is substantially, but not entirely, disclosed by one prior art reference and the differences are of a minor and non-critical nature. Alternatively, your idea can be considered obvious if individual elements of your idea are found in different, but technically related, prior art references and it can be considered obvious to combine the individual elements of the prior art references in a manner to make your idea or invention.

"Non-obvious-ness" is one of the most difficult concepts of patent law.

Going back to our idea for a widget, you have found one patent reference which discloses a widget made of parts A, B, and D, but not C. You must ask yourself, is part C a critical component of your widget and, if so, is there anything in the general knowledge of widgets which would suggest to someone that part C should be included even though is not in the patent reference. If part C is not a critical component, then the patent reference probably renders your idea obvious. If part C is a critical component and there is nothing in the general knowledge of widgets to suggest the inclusion of part C, your idea is probably non-obvious.

The second type of obviousness problem lies where one or more elements of your idea are found in different, related prior art references. In the above example, instead of finding one patent reference, you have found three prior art references. The first reference discloses a widget with parts A, D, E and F. The second reference discloses a widget with parts B, G and H. The third reference discloses a gidget, which has the same function as a widget, but operates differently, with parts C, Y and Z. First you must determine whether all three prior art references relate to similar types of articles. In this case they do. Then you must determine whether each of the elements of your widget idea, A, B, C and D, are found in the prior art references. Again, they are. Finally, you must ask whether anything in the references or commonly known to suggest to suggest that parts A and D of the first reference could be combined with part B from the second reference and with part C of the third reference. If there is nothing to suggest the combination of A, B, C, and D, then your idea is probably not obvious in view of the three prior art references. If, on the other hand, there is something to suggest the combination, you must ask whether combining parts A, B, C and D into one of the widgets or gidgets disclosed in the prior art references would destroy the functionality of the device. If so, then your idea is probably not obvious.

Whether your idea is not obvious must be resolved by first identifying each feature of your idea and finding one or more of those features in the patents uncovered by your search. Then you must ask a series of questions to determine either the obviousness of a change to one of the references to incorporate an element, or the obviousness of combining individual elements in different patents into each of the devices disclosed in each of the patents. These questions should include:

Whether your idea is not obvious must be resolved by first identifying each feature of your idea.

- What are each of the elements of my idea?

- What are the unique elements or features of my idea?

- Do the references all relate to my idea?

- Which references show or describe one or more of the elements of my idea?

- What are the elements?

- Do any of the references show or describe the elements combined in a manner similar to my idea?

- Are any of the elements of my idea missing?

- Can the elements in the references be combined without destroying the functioning of the device or process described in the reference?

- For any missing elements, are those elements something which is already well known?

- Would it have been obvious to me to combine the various elements to arrive at the device or process of my idea?

There are no absolutes in determining non-obviousness. Simply put, it is a judgment call which requires careful review of the references and plenty of thought and consideration.

The importance of a good, thorough patent search cannot be over-emphasized. In addition to the screening benefits of a patent search, searching your idea has the additional advantages of: 1) uncovering patents which may be infringed if you market or sell your invention, which affords you the opportunity to avoid potential infringement problems by either re-designing your invention or by obtaining a license to the patent; and 2) The search aids in your efforts to prepare a patent application, draft

The importance of a good, thorough patent search cannot be over-emphasized.

patent claims and disclose and distinguish the relevant prior art to the patent office.

Applying for a Patent

One does not have to actually make an invention before filing the patent application. Constructing a prototype, or actually "reducing the invention to practice," may help work out many kinks in the invention. You might even find that the process of constructing a prototype results in an entirely different and better approach to the invention.

Keep in mind that any public disclosure or sales of the invention starts a time clock running.

It is essential that you file a patent application if you want to get a patent. When you file your patent application is up to you. Keep in mind that any public disclosure or sales of the invention, including an offer to sell the invention, starts a time clock running. Under the U.S. Patent Laws, all inventors are entitled to a one-year grace period from the date of public disclosure or sale of the invention. This one-year period is termed a "statutory bar" or "bar date." If a patent application for the invention is not filed before the one-year elapses, no valid patent can issue for the invention. Essentially, if you fail to file an application within the one-year grace period, the invention should be considered abandoned. The one-year grace period provides inventors with a period of time to try to promote or commercialize the invention before filing a patent application. A patent application is an expensive and time consuming project.

If you elect to prepare and file your own patent application you should expect to spend many, many hours writing the application and writing patent claims. If you retain a patent attorney or agent you should expect to spend between $1,500 and $2,500 in legal fees for the most basic utility patent application. In addition to this, don't forget that the United States Patent and Trademark Office requires a filing fee of at least $355 for a utility application. These expenses only get you to the point of having the patent application filed with the United States Patent and Trademark Office. Additional legal fees and Patent Office costs will undoubtedly be incurred during the processing or prosecution of the patent application. Many inventors, especially those who use savings or loans to pay for the patent application, use the grace period to get a feel for the commercial value of their idea before committing substantial resources to the project.

Many inventors use the grace period to get a feel for the commercial value of their idea.

There are disadvantages to waiting. The most important of these is that any type of public disclosure before filing the patent application will, for the most part, result in a loss of an ability to obtain foreign patent protection. This happens irrespective of where the disclosure is made. Most foreign countries operate patent systems which rely upon a novelty standard which is absolute; it does not permit **any** prior public disclosure of the invention. Another major disadvantage of prior disclosure of your invention is that potential competitors will have the ability to review your idea at a very early stage and prepare other, possibly improved, versions of your idea, enter the market and dilute your potential market. Worse yet, they could simply copy your idea until you actually obtain your patent. Clearly, the decision not only to file a patent application, but when the application should be filed is important.

The purpose of the patent application is to fully describe and define the subject matter regarded as the invention. The patent ultimately granted by the U.S. Patent and Trademark Office arises entirely out of the patent application originally filed, plus any amendments made to the application during the prosecution of the application.

The patent application contains a specification which fully describes the invention in a manner sufficient to enable one skilled in the art to practice the invention upon expiration of the term. The specification must also disclose the best mode known to the inventor for making the invention at the time the application is filed.

The patent application must also contain at least one patent claim. Patent claims are definitions of the invention. Patent claims define the subject matter of the invention and serve as the metes and bounds of the legal rights conferred by the patent. A patent claim will recite the structural or functional elements of the invention, or the method steps for a process. Additional language concerning the structural or functional relationship between elements or method steps is usually included to clarify how the article or method operates. As with any other definition, the language in a patent claim can be quite broad or can be very specific. It is beneficial to attempt to obtain as broad a definition of the invention as is possible in view of the prior art references.

In addition to the specification and at least one patent claim, the inventor must execute an oath or declaration stating that the invention is the original and that he is the true inventor of the claimed subject matter. A Power of Attorney, Assignment Agreement, and Petition for Small Entity Status, are usually filed where appropriate.

Filing the Application with the U.S. Patent and Trademark Office

The patent application is filed with the U.S. Patent and Trademark Office and receives a filing date and application serial number. The filing date establishes the effective filing date of the application, which serves as an invention priority date, and stops the running of any statutory bar periods, such as the grace period for commercialization or public disclosure. The application serial number serves to identify the patent application during handling at the U.S. Patent and Trademark Office.

A filing fee for the application must be paid at the time the patent application is filed. The U.S. Patent and Trademark Office has a schedule of fees for filing and prosecution of patent applications. A current fee schedule is found in Appendix D. These fees do change frequently. Be sure to check the correct fees before sending anything to the Patent Office.

A patent application must be have a supporting Declaration of each inventor. A Declaration form is found at Appendix E. The primary purpose of the Declaration is to state that the inventors believe themselves to be the true inventors of the invention described in the patent application.

Where the inventor is an independent inventor and is not under any legal obligation to

The inventor must execute an oath stating that he is the true inventor of the claimed subject matter.

23

assign the invention to another person or to a company having over 500 employees, the inventor is entitled to reduced filing fees. In order to qualify for a reduction in filing fees, the inventor must establish that he is a "small entity." This is accomplished by completing and filing a Small Entity Declaration, such as that found in Appendix F. Different types of Small Entity Declarations are available for small businesses and non-profit organizations.

In order to qualify for a reduction in filing fees, the inventor must establish that he is a "small entity."

Finally, the entire patent application, declarations and filing fee should be sent to the U.S. Patent and Trademark Office with a Transmittal Letter. The purpose of the Transmittal Letter, found in Appendix G, is to list the items being enclosed and assist in calculating the appropriate filing fees. It is advisable to enclose a self-addressed stamped post card identifying all items enclosed with the Transmittal Letter. When the Patent Office receives your application, it will stamp the card with both the filing date and the application serial number and return the card to you. This card is an unofficial record of their receipt of your application and should be filed away for safekeeping.

Patent Office Examination of the Application

Once filed, the Application is assigned a preliminary classification according to its subject matter and assigned to an Art Unit and to a Patent Examiner. Patent Examiners are either attorneys or non-attorneys having a particular scientific or technical background in a particular field.

The Patent Examiner's job is to review and evaluate the patent application. The Examiner's review of the application has two basic purposes. The first purpose is to determine whether the inventor's description and disclosure of the invention is adequate to teach how to make or practice the invention and whether the best mode for practicing the invention, known to the inventor, has been disclosed. It is a basic premise of patent law that a patent will be granted only in exchange for a full and fair disclosure of the invention. This allows the invention to be useful to others after the patent is expired.

It is a basic premise of patent law that a patent will be granted only in exchange for a full and fair disclosure of the invention.

Akin to the requirement that an inventor make a full disclosure of the invention, is the legal duty to disclose all prior art known to the inventor which bears on the patentability of the invention. Failure to comply with the duty of disclosure can result in the subsequent invalidity of an issued patent. An Information Disclosure Citation form, found at Appendix H, is useful for disclosing prior art references to the Patent Office.

The second purpose of the Examiner's review is to determine patentability of the invention defined by the patent claims. The Examiner conducts his own patent search to determine the scope and content of the prior art. Based upon his evaluation of the prior art, the Examiner reviews the patent claims and determines whether the subject matter defined in the claims satisfies the utility, novelty and non-obviousness requirements in view of the prior art.

If the Examiner determines that the specification does not meet with the disclosure and best mode requirements, or that the claims lack utility, novelty or are obvious in view of the prior art, the Examiner will issue an Office Action. The Office Action either objects to the specification or claims, or rejects the claims for specified reasons. The applicant has an opportunity to respond to the Office Action by making amendments to the specification and claims. The amendments must not add any new matter into the application, and should be filed with factual, technical or legal arguments. Multiple Office Actions and Applicant responses may ensue until the issues are clarified and the claims deemed allowable or finally rejected.

If the application is in condition for allowance, a patent issues upon payment of an Issue Fee. If the application is finally rejected, the Applicant may appeal the Examiner's determination, abandon the application, or continue the application by filing a continuation application.

A diagram illustrating a typical course of patent prosecution is found at Appendix I.

The protection afforded by a patent is determined principally by the patent claims.

Maintenance fees must be paid 3, 7 and 11 years from the issue date of the patent in order to keep the patent in force. Failure to pay the maintenance fees will result in the patent lapsing and the invention being dedicated to the public.

What Protection Does My Patent Provide?

Protection is for the U.S. and its territories and possessions. The protection afforded by a patent is determined principally by the patent claims. Where ambiguities exist in the claim language, the language will be interpreted with reference to the specification. The patent claims are read literally and in view of the specification.

The term "patent pending" does not give any rights. Rather, it only means is that at the time the notice was placed on the product, a patent application was pending in the Patent and Trademark Office. The notice is placed on products which are marketed to deter copying of the product by others in the marketplace. Since there are no rights until a patent is issued by the U.S. Patent and Trademark Office, there are no rights which can be infringed by someone else copying your invention. A pending patent application cannot be infringed.

A patent is infringed if at least one patent claim literally reads on the accused device or process, or its functional equivalents are substituted for the literally defined claim elements.

Obtaining a patent for your invention does not mean that you do not infringe on an earlier issued patent. Be careful to distinguish between issues of patentability and issues of infringement. The U.S. Patent and Trademark Office only determines issues of patentability, i.e., utility, novelty and non-obviousness, in view of the prior art. Even if the prior art includes a patent which is still in force, the patent examiner will neither consider nor notify you that your invention may infringe upon this prior patent. Issues of infringement relate only to whether the patent claims of an issued patent can be read on to the device or process thought to infringe the patent.

Obtaining a patent for your invention does not mean that you do not infringe on an earlier issued patent.

Exhibit E is a flow diagram reflecting post-issuance litigation possibilities and appeals from the U.S. Patent and Trademark Office.

A patent can be infringed only if the claims in the patent can be construed to "read on" the infringing article or process. Simply put, if you believe an article or process infringes your patent, you must compare the language of each of the patent claims with the article or process and determine whether the language of the claims covers the article or process. In determining whether a patent claim reads on an article or process, there are two general approaches to determining infringement: 1) literal patent infringement, and 2) infringement under the Doctrine of Equivalents.

Literal patent infringement occurs where the device or process thought to infringe incorporates each and every one of the claimed elements as literally set forth in the language of the patent claim. Infringement under the Doctrine of Equivalents occurs where the accused device or process accomplishes substantially the same purpose in substantially the same way and with substantially the same elements as are recited in the patent claims.

One can only infringe a patent by making, using or selling an article or process which is covered by the claims of an unexpired patent. In addition, if you assist someone else in making, using or selling an article or process which is covered by a patent, you may be liable as a contributory infringer.

The patent laws require patent owners to provide notice of the existence of their patent and their position that you may infringe their patent. Notice typically comes by way of a letter from an attorney or by receiving a legal complaint filed with a United States District Court.

Either way, such claims are serious and must not be ignored.

If you are on the receiving end of either a notice letter or a complaint, your potential liability includes being subject to a court order, (either a preliminary injunction or a temporary restraining order) requiring you to discontinue all activities in connection with the patented article or process, and/or to pay monetary damages. The patent statutes allow a patent owner to recover monetary damages "adequate to compensate for the infringement but in no event less than a reasonable royalty for the use made of the invention by the infringer, together with interest and costs as fixed by the court." The court may also increase damages up to three times the amount assessed. The reasonable royalty serves as the floor below which the damages award must not fall. The Court may award greater damages based upon the infringer's profits, the actual damages proven, and whether the infringement was willful.

Patent enforcement and licensing is extremely complex and should not be undertaken without an experienced attorney.

Patent enforcement and licensing is extremely complex and should not be undertaken without an attorney experienced in these matters. A diagram illustrating the various agencies and courts which may become involved in enforcing a patent is found at Appendix J.

CHAPTER THREE
TRADEMARKS AND SERVICE MARKS

What is a Trademark?

A businessman's dream is to have his product readily identified by its trademark. The value of the trademarks "Xerox" for photocopying and "Kleenex" for tissues is readily apparent.

Trademarks are used to protect names and symbols that are used to identify products. These can be registered under state or federal law. A state trademark provides protection only in the state in which the mark is registered. A federal registration provides protection for a trademark throughout the United States. Registration of a trademark provides protection to the trademark owner against competitors who may try to use the trademark owner's reputation to sell their competing products.

The procedure for obtaining protection for a new trademark usually begins with a search. The search aids in making a determination that no one else has registered the same or similar mark. Once availability of the mark is determined, the registration process can begin. Registration of a trademark ensures the maximum available legal protection is obtained.

Registration of a trademark ensures the maximum legal protection is obtained.

Like copyrights, a trademark owner acquires basic trademark protection simply by using his trademark on or in connection with his goods. Registration of a trademark provides additional legal protection. This protection can be especially important if it is ever necessary to file a lawsuit to protect your trademark.

Unlike copyrights, there is no fixed time limit to trademark protection. As long as a business is using a trademark to help sell its goods, it has trademark protection. The registration procedures provide that the registrations be periodically renewed. Trademark protection only terminates when the trademark is no longer used.

A trademark can be a word, name, symbol, device, or any combination thereof to identify and distinguish the goods of a manufacturer or merchant from goods manufactured or sold by others, and to indicate the source of the goods. A mark with these characteristics and functions used in connection with the rendering of services is called a service mark. Such marks are often referred to as "brand names" or "logos"; slogans are also widely used as marks.

A trademark can be a word, name, symbol, device, or any combination thereof.

Many owners of unregistered marks use the ™ (for trademark) or ᴿᴹ (for service mark) symbols, as appropriate, in connection with the marks to indicate their claims of ownership. The ® symbol should be used only after a federal registration has been issued from the Patent and Trademark Office. While owners of marks may acquire rights in their marks under the "common law," they often seek to register their marks because of the procedural and legal advantages obtained through registration with the Patent and Trademark Office.

How Do I Get a Trademark?

Trademark rights come into existence simply by using the mark on or in connection with your product or service. The common law rights which arise by such use are limited to the market areas in which you use the mark. These market areas may be geographical encompassing an entire city, a state, a series of states or the entire country. A market area is not the same as a geographical area; it can also be as small as your neighborhood.

Before using a mark, it is advisable to determine whether someone else is either using the same or similar mark for the same or similar goods or services. This can be accomplished by conducting a search to determine the existence of such marks.

Trademark searching can be quite simple or very complex. There are many sources which list names used for products and business. These sources include the records at the United States Patent and Trademark Office, the registration records maintained by each state government, trade names indexes, business names indexes, the Yellow Pages in each metropolitan area, business directories, trade journals, etc. Many of these sources are available both in book form at public libraries or are available as computer databases which are accessible for a fee to anyone having a modem.

Conducting a search will tell you only whether there are identical or similar names and what the marks are used for.

Conducting a search will tell you only whether there are identical or similar names and what the marks are used for. It is advisable to retain an attorney to conduct a trademark search and provide you with a legal opinion concerning the availability of your mark. There are many instances where people use a name and invest a lot of money in letterhead, business cards, labels, molds or advertising, only to have a trademark owner require them to change the name. Like patents, whether you **intended** to infringe on someone else's trademark rights is irrelevant.

Once you have determined that the name is available, you should start to use the name and then register the name either with the appropriate state agency or with the United States Patent and Trademark Office. Registration places your claim to the name on a publicly available record. At the United States Patent and Trademark Office, both pending registration applications and issued registrations are available for searching. Filing for and obtaining a registration for your mark serves as notice to others that you claim rights to that name.

Obtaining a registration for your mark serves as notice to others that you claim rights to that name.

All states and the federal government provide registration systems for trademarks.

How Do I Register the Trademark?

Registering a mark with the appropriate state agency or the United States Patent and Trademark Office is a relatively easy process. Forms are available from the state agency office in your state, typically the Secretary of State, and from the U.S. Patent and Trademark Office. Most states do not have as rigorous an examination process as the U.S. Patent and Trademark Office. Accordingly, obtaining a state registration is usually much faster than obtaining a federal registration.

State registration of a mark requires that you actually use the mark in the state in which you seek the registration. This requirement parallels the common law rights, but extends them to include the entire state, rather than a smaller market area within the state. For example, if a trademark owner is only selling his products in Scottsdale, Arizona, the common law rights may only provide protection within the city of Scottsdale. However, obtaining a registration for the mark from the State of Arizona will afford protection throughout the State of Arizona, regardless of whether the products are actually sold throughout the state.

Federal registration of a mark also requires that you actually use the mark. You must be using the mark in "interstate commerce." The requirement of use in interstate commerce means that you must either be marketing or selling your goods or services across state lines or be marketing or selling your goods or services in a manner which affects interstate commerce. For example, if the trademark owner in Scottsdale, Arizona is selling his products only in the city of Scottsdale, but sells his products at baseball spring training games or at a resort hotel he may be selling in interstate commerce. This is the case because consumers from out of state are purchasers of the goods in Arizona; thus the sales activity affects interstate commerce. Use in interstate commerce can also involve the direct selling or marketing of goods or services across state lines. If the trademark owner in Scottsdale publishes a mail order catalog which is mailed out of Arizona into California, sells the goods at a trade show in California or opens a sales outlet in California, such activities constitute use in interstate commerce.

Once you obtain a federal registration for your mark, the registration protects your mark throughout the country. This protection does

Federal registration of a mark also requires that you actually use the mark in "interstate commerce."

not depend upon the markets or geographical areas in which you are actually using the mark. Additionally, an issued federal registration is presumed to be valid and establishes valid trademark rights to the mark. Both factors are tremendous advantages for enforcing your trademark rights.

The United States Trademark Laws, found in Title 15 of the United States Code, implement a federal registration scheme for trademarks, service marks, collective marks and certification marks. As discussed earlier, a trademark is a mark used in connection with goods or products, and a service mark is a mark used in connection with rendering of services. Collective marks and certification marks are not as common. A collective mark is a mark used to indicate a group or association of producers as the source of the goods or services; for example, the Florida Citrus Grower's Association. A certification mark is a mark used to indicate approval of the product by a certain company or group of companies; for example, the "UL" mark for approval by Underwriter's Laboratories.

A federal registration establishes valid trademark rights.

The United States Trademark Laws provide for two types of registration: principal registration and supplemental registration. Correspondingly, the United States Patent and Trademark Office maintains a Principal Register and a Supplemental Register of trademarks and service marks. The Principal Register is reserved for marks which are inherently capable of identifying the goods or service. Such marks must be arbitrary, fanciful and not descriptive of the goods or services they identify. Registration on the Principal Register gives its owner a presumption of trademark validity. The Supplemental Register is reserved for marks which are descriptive, but are capable of acquiring "secondary meaning" by identifying the goods or services to consumers. Unlike a Principal Register registration, registration on the Supplemental Register does not afford a presumption of validity for the trademark.

To apply to register a mark with the United States Patent and Trademark Office, the owner must actually be using the mark or have a *bona fide* intention to use the mark in interstate commerce. The registration process is started by filing an application to register the mark with the United States Patent and Trademark Office. Forms registration applications are available from the United States Patent and Trademark Office. An example of such a form is found at Appendix K. The application and registration process is outlined in the flow chart found at Appendix L.

An application to register the mark based upon a prior actual commercial use must state the following:

- that the mark is being used in interstate commerce;

- the date on which the mark was first used anywhere;

- the date on which the mark was first used in interstate commerce;

- the types of goods or services for which the mark is used;

To register a mark with the U.S. Patent and Trademark Office, the owner must actually be using the mark.

- the manner in which the mark is used in connection with the goods or services; and

- the proper International Classification for the goods or services.

The application must be filed with specimens or examples of how you are using the mark. Appropriate specimens include labels, packaging, the actual product, advertising for the services, photographs of the product illustrating the mark on the product, etc. The specimens must show how the mark is affixed to the goods or used in connection with the goods or services. Copies of advertisements for products are **not** considered appropriate specimens for a trademark application.

Copies of advertisements are not considered appropriate specimens for a trademark application.

An application to register the mark based upon a *bona fide* intention to use the mark must state the following:

- that the owner has a *bona fide* intention to use the mark in interstate commerce;

- the types of goods or services for which the mark is used;

- the manner in which the mark will be used on or in connection with the goods or services; and

- the proper International Classification for the goods or services.

Since there has been no actual commercial use of the mark, no specimens are filed with an intent-to-use registration application.

Both an actual use and an intent-to-use registration application must contain a separate sheet including a drawing of the mark. If the mark does not include graphical characters or designs, the drawing may simply be a typewritten representation of the mark. If the mark includes any graphical characters, including a combination of upper and lowercase lettering, or a graphical design, the mark must be submitted as a pen and ink drawing with the drawing not exceeding dimensions of 4 inches by 4 inches.

Additionally, both actual use and intent-to-use registration applications must be filed with a declaration, signed by the owner, stating that he believes to be the exclusive owner of the mark and that the statements made in the application are believed to be true.

Applications must be filed with a declaration that the owner believes to be the exclusive owner of the mark.

Finally, the registration application must be accompanied by an application fee of $245 per International Class identified in the application. Where the goods or services identified in the application fall within more than one International Class, all classes should be identified and a fee paid for each class. Such "multi-class applications" can be filed on a single application.

Each application filed with the United States Patent and Trademark Office is assigned to a "Law Office" at the Patent and Trademark Office and to an Examining Trademark Attorney within the Law Office. The Examining Trademark Attorney examines the application for compliance with technical requirements and to determine whether the mark is "registrable" under the terms of the United States Trademark Laws. The Examining Trademark Attorney will conduct a search to determine whether there are any federal registrations or pending applications for marks which may be identical or likely to be confusingly similar to a consumer.

If the Examining Trademark Attorney finds either an identical or a confusingly similar mark, he issues an Office Action rejecting the registration application. The applicant has the opportunity to respond to the Office Action by amending the application or presenting legal arguments why the two marks are not confusingly similar. If, in the case of an intent-to-use application, you have begun commercial use of the mark, it is possible to amend the application to an actual use application by filing an amendment to allege use and paying a filing fee. Once the Examining Trademark Attorney determines that the application is acceptable and the mark registrable, the application is allowed and sent to the Publication Branch of the U.S. Patent and Trademark Office for publication in the Trademark Official Gazette.

Once the mark is found registrable, the application is published in the Trademark Official Gazette.

The Trademark Official Gazette is a weekly publication of the U.S. Patent and Trademark Office and identifies all allowed applications. Copies of the Trademark Official Gazette can be found at the Patent and Trademark Depository Libraries listed in Appendix C. The purpose of publication is to provide an opportunity, for a period of 30 days from the date of publication, for persons who believe that they may be injured by registration of the mark, to file an opposition to the registration. If no one files an opposition to the registration, and the application is an actual use application, the registration will issue automatically 12 weeks from the date of publication of the mark in the Official Gazette. If no one files an opposition to the registration, and the application is an intent-to-use application, the applicant must file a Statement of Use stating:

- that the mark is being used in interstate commerce;

- the date on which the mark was first used anywhere;

- the date on which the mark was first used in interstate commerce;

- the types of goods or services for which the mark is used; and

- the manner in which the mark is used in connection with the goods or services.

A Statement of Use form is found at Appendix M.

The Statement of Use must be filed within six months from the date of a Notice of Allowance issued by the U.S. Patent and Trademark Office. A filing fee of $100 per International Class must accompany the Statement of Use. If the mark has not been used during the six month period, extensions of time are possible, but an application for the extension and an extension fee must be filed in order to maintain the application in force. An Extension Request form is found at Appendix N.

If an opposition is filed, the registration is postponed pending resolution of the opposition.

If an opposition is filed in either an actual use or an intent-to-use application, the application is transferred to the Trademark Trial and Appeal Board of the United States Patent and Trademark Office, and the registration is postponed pending resolution of the opposition. Whether or not the registration issues depends entirely upon the outcome of the opposition.

The entire registration process takes approximately 13 months for applications based on actual "use in commerce." Once the registration is issued by the Patent and Trademark Office, it is good for a term of ten years. To keep the registration in force, you must file an affidavit or declaration of continued use between the fifth and sixth years after registration. This affidavit or declaration must be supported by additional specimens showing how you are continuing to use the mark. Registrations can be renewed for subsequent ten year periods indefinitely. The only requirement is that you have been and are continuously using the mark.

How Do I Keep My Trademark?

Keep using it! Whether or not you have registered the trademark with a state agency of the U.S. Patent and Trademark Office, you maintain your trademark rights by continuously using the mark. If you stop using the mark there is a risk that the period of non-use may be deemed an abandonment of the mark. In fact, non-use for a period of two or more years is presumed to indicate an intention to abandon the mark!

If you stop using the mark there is a risk that the period of non-use may be deemed an abandonment.

Like patent rights, trademark rights should be enforced. Enforcement of trademark rights may occur through licensing rights under the mark to others or filing lawsuits to stop infringing uses of the trademark. A decision not to enforce your trademark rights can result in substantial dilution of not only your market and, therefore, your revenues, but also the trademark rights afforded by either your use or registration of the mark.

What do fabric patterns, board games and newspapers have in common? Music, books, and computer software? They are all protected by a copyright. All original works of authorship are protected by copyright laws.

The copyright laws of the United States give the copyright owner a series of exclusive rights to the work. These rights permit the owner to use or allow others to use the work in a wide variety of ways.

A business owns the copyright to works created by its employees. However, a business should be careful about the use of independent contractors or temporary personnel. The law provides that the copyright to a work created by an independent contractor for another person is owned by the independent contractor unless there is a written agreement providing for the business to be the owner of the copyright.

Works of authorship automatically have a copyright simply by being created. This provides

> *Works of authorship automatically have a copyright simply by being created.*

the author with some basic copyright protection. In order to further protect a work and your copyright, a copyright notice should appear in a conspicuous place. The notice should include the word "copyright" or © symbol, the year of the first publication and the name of the copyright owner. An example is shown on page 49. Another step for protecting a copyright is registering the work with the United States Copyright Office in Washington, D.C.

A copyright in a work lasts for the lifetime of the author of the work plus fifty years. For corporations, the copyright is for seventy-five years from the first publication of the work, or one hundred years from creation of the work.

Copyrights should be registered in order to provide maximum protection for a work. Copyrights are valuable because they give their owners the exclusive right to use, reproduce and charge for reproducing the copyrighted work.

What is a Copyright?

A copyright in a work lasts for the lifetime of the author plus fifty years.

Copyright is a form of protection provided by the United States Copyright Act. Copyrights protect "original works of authorship" including literary, dramatic, musical, artistic, and certain other intellectual works. This protection is available to authors of both published and unpublished works.

The Copyright Act generally gives the owner of copyright the exclusive right to do and to authorize others to do the following:

To reproduce the copyrighted work in copies or phonorecords;

To prepare derivative works based upon the copyrighted work;

To distribute copies or phonorecords of the copyrighted work to the public by sale or other transfer of ownership, or by rental, lease, or lending;

To perform the copyrighted work publicly, in the case of literary, musical, dramatic, and choreographic works, pantomimes, and motion pictures and other audiovisual works, and

To display the copyrighted work publicly, in the case of literary, musical, dramatic, and choreographic works, pantomimes, and pictorial, graphic, or sculptural works, including the individual images of a motion picture or other audiovisual work.

A copyright owner's exclusive rights do have exceptions. In some cases, these limitations are specified exemptions from copyright liability. One major limitation is the doctrine of "fair use." In other instances, the limitation takes the form of a "compulsory license" under which certain limited uses of copyrighted works are permitted upon payment of specified royalties and compliance with statutory conditions.

How Do I Get a Copyright?

Copyright protection exists from the time the work is created in fixed form: that is, it is incident of the process of authorship. The copyright in the work of authorship **immediately** becomes the property of the author who created it. Only the author or those deriving their rights through the author can rightfully claim copyright.

Only the author or those deriving their rights through the author can rightfully claim copyright.

An employer is considered the author and owner of a work created by an employee. This type of work is considered a "work made for hire" if either of the following conditions are satisfied: 1) The work is prepared by an employee within the scope of the employment; or 2) The work was specially ordered or commissioned for use as a contribution to a collective work, as part of a motion picture or other audiovisual work, as a translation, as a supplementary work, as a compilation, as an instructional text, as a test, as answer material for a test, or as an atlas, if the parties expressly agree in a written instrument signed by them that the work will be considered a work made for hire.

The authors of a joint work are co-owners of the copyright in the work, unless there is an agreement to the contrary.

Owning either a copy or an original of a copyrighted work, such as a book, manuscript or painting does not give you any rights under the copyright laws. Owning any material object which embodies a protected work does not of itself give any rights in the copyright.

What is Copyrightable?

The authors of a joint work are co-owners of the copyright unless there is an agreement to the contrary.

Copyright protects "original works of authorship" that are fixed in a tangible form of expression. The fixation need not be directly perceptible, so long as it may be communicated with the aid of a machine or device. Copyrightable works include the following categories:

- Literary works

- Musical works, including any accompanying words

- Dramatic works, including any accompanying music

- Pantomimes and choreographic works

- Pictorial, graphic, and sculptural works

- Motion pictures and other audiovisual

works

- Sound recordings

These categories should be viewed quite broadly. For example, computer programs are considered "literary works" and architectural blueprints are "pictorial, graphic, and sculptural works."

Several categories of material are generally **not** eligible for statutory copyright protection. These include:

Works that *have not been fixed in a tangible form.* For example, choreographic works that have not been notated or recorded, or improvisational speeches or performances that have not been written or recorded.

Titles, names, short phrases, and slogans; familiar symbols or designs; mere variations of typographic ornamentation, lettering, or coloring; mere listings of ingredients or contents.

Ideas, procedures, methods, systems, processes, concepts, principles, discoveries, or devices, as distinguished from a description, explanation, or illustration.

Works consisting entirely of information that is *common property* and containing no original authorship. For example: standard calendars, height and weight charts, tape measures and rulers, and lists or tables taken from public documents or other common sources.

How Do I Get a Copyright?

Obtaining copyright protection for a work which you create is one of the most frequently misunderstood processes. No publication or registration or other action in the Copyright Office is required to secure copyright.

Copyright arises **automatically** and **immediately** when the work is created, and a work is "created" when it is fixed in a copy or phonorecord for the first time. In general, "copies" are material objects from which a work can be read or visually perceived either directly or with the aid of a machine or device, such as books, manuscripts, sheet music, film, videotape, or microfilm. "Phonorecords" are material objects embodying fixations of sounds (excluding, by statutory definition, motion picture soundtracks), such as digital audio tapes, compact discs, cassette tapes, or records. Thus, a song (the "work") can be fixed as lyrics or words in sheet music ("copies") or recorded on a compact disc or vinyl record ("phonorecords"), or both.

Copyright arises automatically and immediately when the work is created.

Once a work has been created, the work may be published or remain unpublished. The Copyright Act defines publication as follows:

"PUBLICATION" IS THE DISTRIBUTION OF COPIES OR PHONORECORDS OF A WORK TO THE PUBLIC BY SALE OR OTHER TRANSFER OF OWNERSHIP, OR BY RENTAL, LEASE, OR LENDING. THE OFFERING TO DISTRIBUTE COPIES OR PHONORECORDS TO A GROUP OF PERSONS FOR PURPOSES OF FURTHER DISTRIBUTION, PUBLIC PERFORMANCE, OR PUBLIC DISPLAY, CONSTITUTES PUBLICATION. A PUBLIC PERFORMANCE OR DISPLAY OF A WORK DOES NOT OF ITSELF CONSTITUTE PUBLICATION.

When a work is published, all published copies should bear a notice of copyright. This is not a legal requirement, but does give notice of the copyright and enhances your ability to enforce the copyright. Works that are published with notice of copyright in the United States are subject to mandatory deposit with the Library of Congress.

The year of publication may determine the duration of copyright protection for anonymous and pseudonymous works (when the author's identity is not revealed in the records of the Copyright Office) and for works made for hire.

Deposit requirements for registration of published works differ from those for registration of unpublished works.

When a work is published with permission from the copyright owner, a copyright notice should be placed on all publicly distributed copies and on all publicly distributed phonorecords of sound recordings. This notice should also be placed on all copies of the work published in foreign countries. Failure to place a copyright notice on published copies does not prevent you from claiming copyright to the work, but does prevent you from claiming certain additional rights.

The use of the copyright notice is the responsibility of the copyright owner.

The use of the copyright notice is the responsibility of the copyright owner and does not require advance permission from, or registration with, the Copyright Office. As mentioned earlier, use of the notice makes the published works subject to mandatory deposit requirements.

The notice for visually perceptible copies should contain all of the following three elements:

(1) The symbol ©, the word "Copyright," or the abbreviation "Copr."

(2) The year of first publication of the work. The year may be omitted where a pictorial, graphic, or sculptural work, with accompanying textual matter is reproduced on greeting cards, postcards, stationery, jewelry, dolls, toys, or any useful article.

(3) The name of the copyright owner or an abbreviation of the name which can be recognized, or a generally known alternative designation of the owner. Initials which are not generally known or recognized are not proper.

Examples:

© 1993 Rosenbaum & Associates, P.C.

Copyright 1993 David G. Rosenbaum

A copyright notice can also be placed on an unpublished work. In this instance, the year should be the year the work was created. When the work is published, the year should be revised to reflect the year of first publication.

A copyright notice can also be placed on an unpublished work.

How Long Does a Copyright Last?

For works created on or after January 1, 1978, the copyright ordinarily lasts for the life of the author plus 50 years. In the case of joint work created by two or more authors the copyright term lasts for 50 years after the last surviving author's death. For works made for hire, and for anonymous and pseudonymous works in which the authors true identity is withheld, the duration of copyright will be 75 years from publication or 100 years from creation of the work, whichever is shorter.

For works published or registered before 1978, the copyright term was 28 years from the registration date. The copyright term was renewable for one subsequent 28 year period. For copyrights existing on January 1, 1978, the current law allows renewal for one 47 year term, thus extending their term to 75 years. A renewal application must be filed with the Copyright Office to secure the renewal term. This renewal application must be filed before the first 28 year term expires.

Do I Need to Register the Copyright?

Registration is beneficial because it establishes a public record of the copyright.

Copyright registration is not required to protect your copyright. Registration is beneficial because it establishes a public record of the copyright, and the copyright law provides for several advantages of registration which encourage owners to register their copyrights.

The advantages of registering the copyright include:

Registration establishes a ***public record*** of the copyright claim;

Registration is ordinarily necessary before any ***infringement suits*** may be filed in court;

If made before publication or within 5 years of publication, registration will establish ***presumptive validity*** of the copyright.

If registration is made within 3 months after publication of the work or prior to an infringement of the work, attorney's fees and statutory damages are recoverable in a lawsuit. Otherwise, only an award of actual damages and profits is available to the copyright owner. Statutory damages allow you to recover up to $20,000 for innocent infringement and up to $100,000 for willful infringement of the copyright. These statutory damages are in lieu of actual damages.

How Do I Register a Copyright?

Copyright registration is quite easy. First, it is necessary to obtain a copyright registration application form from the U.S. Copyright Office in Washington, D.C. These forms are available by writing to the Copyright Office or may be ordered by telephone. Because the forms change from time to time, it is best to obtain the forms directly from the Copyright Office to ensure that you are using the latest version. The forms are:

Form TX: for published and unpublished non-dramatic literary works.

Form SE: for serial works issued or intended to be issued in successive parts bearing numerical or chronological designations and intended to be continued indefinitely (periodicals, newspapers, magazines, newsletters, annuals, journals, etc.).

Form PA: for published and unpublished works of the performing arts (musical and dramatic works, pantomimes and choreographic works, motion pictures and other audiovisual works).

It is best to obtain the forms directly from the Copyright Office to ensure that you are using the latest version.

Form VA: for published and unpublished works of the visual arts (pictorial, graphic, and sculptural works).

Form SR: for published and unpublished sound recordings.

Form RE: for claims to renewal copyright works copyrighted under the law in effect through December 31, 1977 (1909 Copyright Act).

Form CA: for supplementary registration to correct or amplify information given in the Copyright Office record of an earlier registration.

Form GR/CP: for registration of a group of contributions to periodicals in addition to an application Form TX, PA, or VA.

Instructions for completing each form are provided with the forms. It is not necessary for an attorney to represent you in filing the forms. You may, however, find it beneficial to consult with an attorney to assist you with the process.

It is not necessary for an attorney to represent you in filing the forms.

The application must consist of the following:

- A properly completed application form

- A non-refundable filing fee of $20 for each application

- A "deposit" (sample) of the work being registered.

The deposit required depends upon the nature and type of work being registered:

- If the work is unpublished, send *one* complete copy or phonorecord.

- If the work was first published in the

United States on or after January 1, 1978, send *two* complete copies or phonorecords of the best edition.

- If the work was first published in the United States before January 1, 1978, send *two* complete copies or phonorecords of the work as first published.

- If the work was first published outside the United States, whenever published, send *one* complete copy or phonorecord of the work as first published.

Copyright registration applications can be filed by any of the following people:

1) The *author*. Remember, the author may be either the person who created the work or the employer if the work was a "work made for hire."

2) The copyright *claimant*. The copyright claimant is either the author or a person or organization that has obtained ownership of all the rights under the copyright initially belonging to the author.

3) The *owner* of exclusive rights. Any of the exclusive rights which make up a copyright and any subdivision of them can be transferred and owned separately. The term "copyright owner" includes the exclusive owner of any one or more of the exclusive rights which make up a copyright.

4) The duly authorized *agent* of any of the above.

All three items—the application form, the deposit and the fee—must be contained within the same envelope or package and sent to the

Copyright Office. Fees must be in U.S. funds drawn on an American bank and paid by check or money order. The application and materials should be addressed to the Register of Copyrights, Copyright Office, Library of Congress, Washington, D.C. 20559. You should send the package by certified mail with a return receipt requested, or enclose a self-addressed stamped post card itemizing the package enclosures. The Copyright Office will date stamp the post card and return it to you as evidence that they received the application.

Once the Copyright Office receives the complete application, including deposit and fee, the date of receipt is the effective date of the registration. This is the case regardless of how long it takes the Copyright Office to process the application and actually issue the registration certificate.

It usually takes the Copyright Office about 120 days to process the application.

It usually takes the Copyright Office about 120 days from their receipt of the application to process the application. Within 120 days you should expect to receive a letter from an examiner at the Copyright Office if further information is required, or if the application is rejected. If no additional information is required and the application is accepted, the Certificate of Registration is usually mailed within the 120 day time period.

The Copyright Office publishes application forms, informational circulars, regulations and announcements. Copies of these may be obtained by writing or telephoning the Copyright Office.

How Do I Enforce My Copyright?

As with patents and trademarks, copyrights are enforced through either licensing or lawsuits in the federal courts. The exclusive rights afforded by a copyright may be separately licensed either on an exclusive or a non-exclusive basis, or may be licensed as a package. Alternatively, copyrights are enforced by bringing a lawsuit in a United States District Court. The Copyright Act permits the copyright owner to:

Copyrights are enforced through either licensing or lawsuits in the federal courts.

- obtain a court-ordered seizure of all infringing works;

- obtain a temporary restraining order and injunction against further infringement of the copyright;

- recover either actual damages resulting from the infringement or elect to recover statutory damages;

- recover all reasonable attorney's fees and costs of bringing the lawsuit.

Again, like patents and trademarks, copyright licensing and enforcement through court action is extremely complex and should not be undertaken before retaining an attorney experienced in such matters.

Finally, just a few words about another type of intellectual property protection: trade secrets.

A trade secret can consist of any information which gives you an advantage over a competitor and which is not generally known. Examples of information which can be a trade secret include formulas, business plans, customer lists, internal business memoranda, methods of making something, etc. Trade secrets are also generally termed "confidential information" or "proprietary information." Trade secret law is governed by the laws of each state. Many states have enacted a version of the Uniform Trade Secrets Act. This has created a body of substantially uniform laws among the states which have adopted it. The states having some version of the Uniform Trade Secrets Act are listed in Appendix O.

A customary way to protect a trade secret is to enter into a confidentiality agreement.

In order to have a trade secret it is only necessary to have developed some information, whether tangible or intangible, and to have taken reasonable measures to keep the information secret. This does not mean that the information cannot be disclosed. It merely means that you have to take reasonable measures to protect unauthorized disclosures of the information.

A customary way to protect a trade secret, while still disclosing the trade secret to another, is to enter into a contract which obligates the person receiving the information to maintain the information confidential. Such agreements are termed "confidentiality agreements" or "proprietary rights agreements." An example of a very general confidentiality agreement is found at Appendix P. Additionally, where an employee is supplied with trade secret information through his job, an employment agreement can include a provision restricting the employee from disclosing or using the information outside of work. If a party agrees to keep information confidential, and then violates that agreement, the confidentiality agreement can be enforced under a breach of contract claim through the state court system. This remedy may be in addition to or preempted by the trade secret laws of your particular state.

Because a patent requires full disclosure of the invention, before filing a patent application you should consider whether the information or invention is best protected as a trade secret. If the invention is very difficult to "reverse engineer," then trade secret protection may be appropriate, if not better. Trade secrets can last indefinitely, while patents expire after 17 years.

Misappropriation of trade secrets most often occurs in an employment context. This occurs where an employee or an independent contractor who has learned trade secret information leaves the job and takes a new job with a competitor. Clearly, there is a danger that the employee will disclose the information to his new employer. This would likely result in damage to the former employer. Such unauthorized disclosures can be prevented by first obtaining either a good confidentiality agreement with the employee or including a confidentiality provision in an employment contract. Prior to such an employee leaving, there should be an exit inter-

Misappropriation of trade secrets most often occurs in an employment context.

view with the employee to remind him of the contract obligations concerning unauthorized use or disclosure of trade secret information.

It is usually necessary to take immediate legal action to protect against continued disclosure and further dissemination of the trade secret information. Such legal action should include pursuing either a temporary restraining order or a preliminary injunction restricting the employee and his new employer from using or disclosing the trade secret information.

Trade secrets, just like patents, trademarks and copyrights, are property rights.

Trade secrets, just like patents, trademarks and copyrights, are property rights. They can be licensed or assigned to another person or business. The important thing to remember about trade secrets is take the word "secret" seriously. You must take measures to safeguard the secrets; if you don't, the cat will have left the bag!

APPENDIX A

United States Patent [19]

Ferguson

US005116502A

[11] Patent Number: 5,116,502

[45] Date of Patent: May 26, 1992

[54] ELONGATE HOUSING WITH END CAP MEMBERS

[76] Inventor: George E. Ferguson, 7740 E. Glenrosa, No. 112, Scottsdale, Ariz. 85251

[21] Appl. No.: 590,349

[22] Filed: Sep. 27, 1990

[51] Int. Cl.⁵ B01D 27/02; B01D 27/08

[52] U.S. Cl. 210/266; 210/282; 210/420; 210/433.1; 210/453

[58] Field of Search 210/418, 420, 445, 450, 210/451, 453, 449, 266, 282, 284, 433.1, 311

[56] References Cited

U.S. PATENT DOCUMENTS

2,316,206	4/1943	Wilson	210/453
3,043,432	7/1962	Megesi	210/311
3,109,812	11/1963	McAulay	210/460
3,535,235	10/1970	Schouw	210/30
3,595,399	7/1971	Abos	210/266
3,645,402	2/1972	Alexander et al.	210/311
3,900,397	8/1975	Bell	210/128
3,950,253	4/1976	Stern	210/282
3,963,620	6/1976	Vor	210/279
4,049,550	9/1977	Obidniak	210/152
4,211,743	7/1980	Van Meter et al.	210/282
4,271,015	6/1981	Moore	210/94
4,303,521	12/1981	Lehmann	210/282

4,312,754	1/1982	LaFontaine	210/267
4,497,348	2/1985	Sedam	141/2
4,509,569	4/1985	Adolfsson	141/360
4,514,994	5/1985	Mabb	62/389
4,564,126	1/1986	Adolfsson	222/61
4,597,509	7/1986	Pereira	222/129
4,609,466	9/1986	McCausland et al.	210/244
4,693,820	9/1987	Baxter	210/232
4,708,827	11/1987	McMillin	261/35
4,765,906	8/1988	Downing et al.	210/636
4,798,672	1/1989	Knight	210/282
5,021,250	6/1991	Ferguson	426/231

Primary Examiner—Robert A. Dawson
Assistant Examiner—Wanda L. Millard
Attorney, Agent, or Firm—David G. Rosenbaum

[57] ABSTRACT

A horizontal counter-top water filter adapted to reside behind a sink faucet fixture. The water filter has a horizontal housing defining a fluid inlet chamber and a fluid filtration chamber, an inlet end cap which is configured to conduct an incoming fluid flow from the fluid inlet chamber to the fluid filtration chamber and an outlet end cap configured to receive a filtered fluid flow from the fluid filtration chamber to a fluid outlet spigot. The water filter is additionally fitted with a diverter valve and fluid conduit, which conducts diverted fluid from a sink faucet into the water filter.

24 Claims, 2 Drawing Sheets

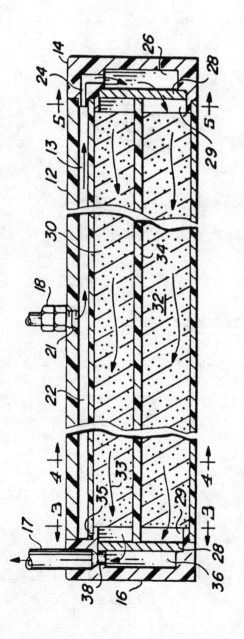

61

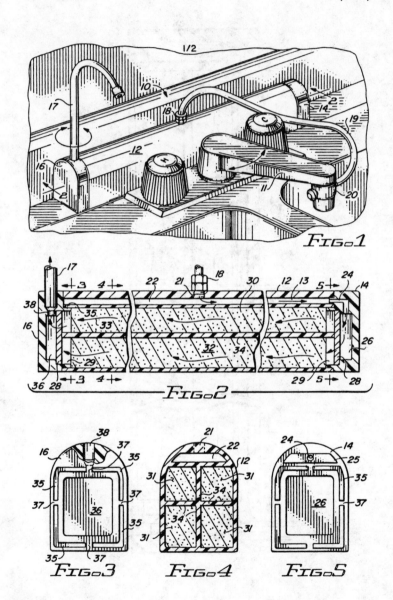

FIG. 1

FIG. 2

FIG. 3   FIG. 4   FIG. 5

62

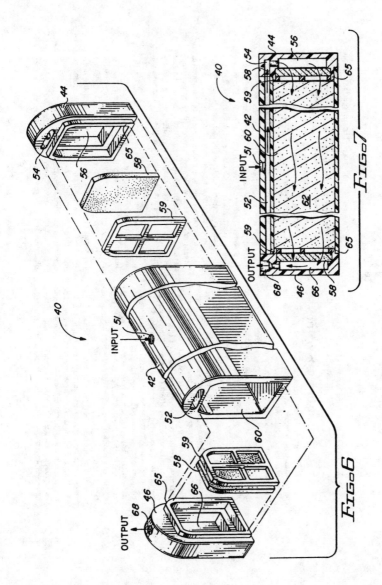

63

1

ELONGATE HOUSING WITH END CAP MEMBERS

BACKGROUND OF THE INVENTION

The present invention relates to a water filtration apparatus which is particularly suited for domestic use to improve the potability of water.

It is a well-known fact that, as population densities increase, it becomes more and more difficult to provide sufficient water of satisfactory purity and potability for domestic use. The purity and quality of drinking water, even from municipal water systems, is increasingly poor and very often unsatisfactory. Furthermore, in addition to industrial and domestic pollution related to high population densities, drinking water in many locations has both a disagreeable odor and aftertaste because of dissolved materials in the water, which, while not necessarily harmful, reduce the potability of the water.

Contaminants which affect the taste of the water are particularly annoying to people who are not residents of the area from where the water is supplied. Additionally, contaminants which affect the taste of the water are particularly annoying when water is used for particular purposes, such as brewing coffee or tea, where the taste of the end product is significantly effected by the contamination.

Because of these factors, a number of filtration devices have been proposed in the past for improving drinking water. However, these prior art devices have been generally ineffective because of deficiencies and inadequacies of design. Most commonly, such filters have employed only one filtration medium, generally

2

easily stored out of the way. The present invention provides a unique water purification system which is particularly well adapted for use as a domestic appliance, which holds several advantages and superior features, which will be appreciated by those skilled in the art upon reading the following description of the invention with reference to its preferred embodiments.

SUMMARY OF THE INVENTION

The present invention provides a water purification system particularly adapted for use in supplying purified water for human internal consumption. The invention is particularly well-adapted for use as a kitchen appliance in connection to a kitchen sink faucet or the like for supplying drinking or cooking water.

In accordance with a broad aspect of the present invention, there is provided a water filter unit characterized by a longitudinal, horizontally disposed filter unit, a water inlet, leading to the filter unit, an adsorbent-type filter medium and an outlet for dispensing a purified and filtered water.

In accordance with a more particular aspect of the present invention, the filtration apparatus includes a horizontally-oriented housing having a centrally disposed inlet, which is in fluid flow communication with a diverter valve attached to a sink faucet. The housing has a pair of end caps which seal the ends of the horizontal filter, conduct an internal fluid flow from the inlet through interior chambers in the housing, and dispense a purified fluid therefrom.

The housing consists generally of a longitudinal inlet chamber and a larger longitudinal filtration chamber

charcoal, and have been limited in effectiveness to remove only those contaminants for which that medium is 35 effective. These contaminants are generally organic materials and odoriferous materials, such as dissolved halogens, which may combine readily with the carbon and the charcoal. However, there are many serious contaminants, such as disease- and illness-causing bacteria, which are not generally removed by charcoal. It 40 has been generally thought that it is necessary, in order to remove bacteria, to boil or distill drinking water for domestic use.

Additionally, many of the domestic water filtration 45 apparatuses are of the countertop type. These generally consist of vertical cylinders which receive water from a diverter valve attached to a sink faucet and introduce unpurified water to the bottom of a charcoal stack, flow the water upward against gravity and dispense the fil- 50 tered water from a spigot located at the top of the charcoal stack. The configuration of these units is bulky and requires that the units be placed adjacent to the sink where they interfere with household tasks of washing dishes, etc. Moreover, the tubing interconnecting the 55 diverter valve and the filtration apparatus is obtrusive and possibly dangerous to those people working near the sink. Accordingly, there has been a continuing need for a water filter system which may be readily adapted for use as a domestic appliance for connection to do- 60 mestic water supplies, which are often considered to be suitable for use for potable water, but which may be dangerously toxic. In this regard, therefore, there has been a long felt need for a water purification system which is easily utilized in conjunction with a household 65 water distribution system, which may be used only when it is necessary to provide a supply of drinking or cooking water, is unobtrusive and may otherwise be

which contains any desirable filter medium or combination of filter media. Each of the end caps seal an end of the horizontal filter and communicate with at least one of the fluid inlet chamber and the filtration chamber. Specifically, an inlet end cap has a fluid conduit, integral with the structure of the end cap, which communicates with the fluid inlet chamber and receives fluid therefrom and conducts the fluid through the end cap body into an opening of the end cap which, in turn, conducts the fluid to be filtered into the filtration chamber. A second end cap, an outlet end cap, has a fluid receiving chamber or recess defined in the back of the outlet end cap which receives filtered fluid from the filtration chamber and communicates with a spigot opening in the outlet end cap body to conduct filtered fluid to a spigot. The outlet end cap is sealed against an end of the fluid inlet chamber, thereby closing the fluid inlet chamber to permit unidirectional flow within the fluid inlet chamber.

These and other objects, features and advantages of the present invention will become more apparent and better understood to those skilled in the art from the following more detailed description of the preferred embodiments of the invention taken with reference to the accompanying drawings, in which like features are identified by like reference numerals.

BRIEF DESCRIPTION OF THE DRAWINGS

FIG. 1 is a perspective view of a sink and faucet arrangement illustrating connection of the water filter of the present invention thereto and the positioning of the water filter relative thereto.

FIG. 2 is a cross-sectional view taken along line 2—2 of FIG. 1.

5,116,502

FIG. 3 is a cross-sectional view taken along line 3—3 of FIG. 2.

FIG. 4 is a cross-sectional view taken along line 4—4 of FIG. 2.

FIG. 5 is a cross-sectional view taken along line 5—5 of FIG. 2.

FIG. 6 is a perspective exploded view of another preferred embodiment of the water filter of the present invention.

FIG. 7 is a side elevational cross-sectional view thereof.

DETAILED DESCRIPTION OF THE PREFERRED EMBODIMENTS

Turning generally to FIG. 1, the water filter 10 of the present invention is illustrated in its intended position in engagement to a sink faucet 11. Generally, the water filter 10 consists of a horizontal housing 12, a pair of end caps 14, 16, an outlet spigot 17 attached to end cap 16, a fluid flow connector 18 connected to tubing 19 which is, in turn, connected to a diverter valve 20, attached to the outlet of the faucet 11. An important aspect of the present invention is that water filter 10 is configured, due to its horizontally elongated shape, to reside in the often unused space immediately behind the faucet 11. The fluid flow connector 18 is optimally positioned generally centrally to the horizontally elongated housing 12 such that it is in general alignment with the axis of the sink faucet 11. Those skilled in the art will appreciate that such a configuration places the water filter 10 away from the vast majority of activity in the sink, thereby eliminating a substantial disadvantage of most countertop units which reside adjacent to the sink due

structural support. The cross-brace members 34 may extend the entire longitudinal length of the chamber or may be otherwise configured to enhance the structural rigidity of housing 12. A second purpose for cross-brace members 34, according to the preferred embodiment of the invention. is to divide filtration chamber 30 into a plurality of smaller flow chambers 31 which provides greater exposure of the fluid to the filter medium 32. By dividing filtration chamber 30 into a plurality of smaller flow sub-chambers 31, fluid entering the filtration chamber 30 is directed into the smaller flow chambers 31 by the cross-brace members 34. Settling of the fluid flow at the bottom of the filtration chamber 30 is inhibited and the fluid flow is exposed to substantially the entire body of fluid filtration medium 32.

There is also provided a fluid inlet end cap 14 and a fluid outlet end cap 16. Fluid inlet end cap 14 conducts a fluid flow 13 from fluid inlet chamber 22 into the filtration chamber 30. Fluid inlet end cap 14 is preferably formed as a single integral body having an inlet end cap receiving chamber 24 and an inlet end cap flow chamber 26. Each of the receiving chamber 24 and flow chamber 26 are formed as openings in the body of inlet end cap 14. Upon assembly with housing 12, inlet end cap receiving chamber 24 is in fluid flow communication with inlet chamber 22 of housing 12, and flow chamber 24 is in fluid flow communication with filtration chamber 30. Inlet end cap receiving chamber 24 receives the fluid flow 13 from inlet chamber 22 and conducts the fluid flow 13 through the body of the inlet end cap 14 into the inlet end cap flow chamber 26. At this point, the fluid flow 13 is positioned to enter the filtration chamber 30.

to their size and vertically upstanding nature. Additionally, this configuration permits user-selection of either a right-handed or left-handed orientation of the spigot 17. An alternative configuration may include displacement of the inlet opening to another point on the longitudinal axis of the housing 12, or leading directly into the end cap 14. These alternative configurations are, however, less desirable as they would require a displaced position of the filter 10 relative to the faucet 11 or compromise filter medium volume.

With reference to FIG. 2, the best mode and preferred embodiment contemplated by the present invention is illustrated in the cross-section. As previously set forth, the water filter consists of three principal components, i.e. housing 12, end cap 14 and end cap 16. Housing 12 consists generally of a fluid inlet chamber 22 which is a longitudinal chamber residing in an upper portion of the longitudinal housing 12. According to the preferred embodiment of the invention, fluid inlet chamber 22 resides immediately adjacent to an upper interior surface of the housing 12 and extends substantially the entire longitudinal aspect of the housing 12. Those skilled in the art will appreciate, however, that it is preferable, for manufacturing purposes, to have fluid inlet chamber 22 extend the entire length of the housing 12. Housing 12 further consists of a filtration chamber 30 in which a filter medium 32 may be disposed. Filtration chamber 30 is a large longitudinally oriented chamber which extends the entire length of the housing 12 and is open on both ends thereof.

Finally, housing 12 has an associated fluid inlet aperture 21 passing through an upper surface thereof which communicates with fluid inlet chamber 22. It is also desirable, but not required, to provide cross-brace members 34 within the fluid filtration chamber 30 to provide

Outlet end cap 16 consists generally of an outlet receiving chamber 36 and a bore 38 in fluid flow communication therewith. As with inlet end cap 14, outlet end cap 16 is preferably formed of a single integral body having openings formed therein which form outlet receiving chamber 36 and spigot receiving bore 38. Outlet receiving chamber 36 is preferably configured in a lateral face of outlet end cap 16 and, when outlet end cap 16 is assembled with housing 12, receives the flow of filtered fluid 33 from the filtration chamber 30 and conducts the filtered fluid flow 33 from the outlet receiving chamber 36 to the bore 38. The filtered fluid flow 33 then exits through bore 38.

A filter member is operably associated with each of the inlet end cap 14 and outlet end cap 16 to prevent particulate matter from entering or leaving the filtration chamber 30 in the inlet fluid flow 13 or the filtered fluid flow 33. The filter member 28 is seated within each of the inlet end cap 14 and outlet end cap 16 adjacent to the filtration chamber 30 and interdisposed between filtration chamber 30 and each of the inlet receiving chamber 26 and outlet receiving chamber 36 of inlet end cap 14 and outlet end cap 16, respectively. According to the best mode contemplated by the invention, but not required in accordance with a preferred embodiment, a filter member retainer 29 is provided in conjunction with each of the filter members 28 which operably engages and retains the filter member 28 in an interference fit with each of the inlet end cap 14 and outlet end cap 16.

Also associated with the water filter 10 are a fluid flow connector 18 which is operably coupled to fluid inlet aperture 21 passing through housing 12 and in fluid flow communication with inlet chamber 22. Fluid connector 18 operably couples the fluid conduit 19 leading

67

from diverter valve 20 to the housing 12 such that unfiltered fluid, diverted by diverter valve 20 from the faucet 11, is conducted through fluid conduit 19 into the inlet chamber 22 of housing 12. A rotatable spigot 17 may be operably disposed in bore 38 to receive the filtered fluid flow 33 and dispense filtered fluid from the spigot 17. It is desirable, though not necessary, to have spigot member 17 be freely rotatable within bore 38 in order to allow reciprocal orientation of the filter apparatus 10 and, thereby, facilitate either right-handed or left-handed orientation of the water filter 10 with reference to the faucet 11. Alternatively, fluid conduit may be operably connected to bore 38 and lead the filtered fluid flow 33 to a two-way diverter valve 20.

Turning now to FIGS. 3–5, there is better illustrated the preferred configurations of outlet end cap 16, filtration chamber 30, and inlet end cap 14, respectively. Outlet end cap 16 is illustrated in FIG. 3. Outlet end cap 16 consists generally of a single body having outlet receiving chamber 36 in fluid flow communication with spigot receiving bore 38. A fluid conduit 37 may be provided between outlet receiving chamber 36 and spigot receiving bore 38 to conduct fluid therebetween. Alternatively, the spigot receiving bore may pass directly through the end cap body 16 to the outlet receiving chamber 36. At least one of a plurality of locking protrusions 35 project laterally from the body of outlet end cap 16 and are generally perpendicular to a longitudinal plane of end cap 16. The configuration of locking protrusions 35 corresponds to the inner peripheral dimensions of filtration chamber 30 such that an interference fit therebetween is achieved. If, as illustrated in FIG. 4, filtration chamber 30 is provided with a plural-

art. According to the preferred embodiment, however, it is desirable to mold end caps 16 and 14 and to extrude housing 12. Extrusion of housing 12 permits formation of the continuous longitudinal inlet chambers 22 and filtration chamber 30. Furthermore, it is desirable, according to the best mode contemplated by the invention, to provide an interference engagement between each of the end caps 14 and 16 and the housing 12 and to ultrasonically or heat weld the end caps 14 and 16 to the housing 12 to provide a fluid tight engagement therebetween. Use of chemical-based adhesives is undesirable due to health and safety regulations issued by the Environmental Protection Agency. Additionally, any acceptable filter medium comporting with the health standards promulgated by the Environmental Protection Agency is contemplated. The filter members 28 are preferably a microporous material, such as a microporous polyethylene material marketed under the trademark POREX, which is die cut or otherwise configured to be engaged by and retained within each of the end caps 14 and 16.

In accordance with a second preferred embodiment of the invention as illustrated with reference to FIGS. 6 and 7, there is provided a filter 40, also consisting of a horizontally oriented longitudinal housing 42 defining an inner fluid inlet chamber 52 which extends the entire lengthwise aspect of the chamber of the housing 42 and a filtration chamber 60 for receiving and containing a filtration medium 62. Housing 42 also has an associated input aperture 51 substantially centrally disposed along the lengthwise aspect and in an upper peripheral surface thereof which communicates with the fluid inlet chamber 52. End caps 44 and 46 are provided and which

ity of cross-brace members **34**, it may be necessary to also provide at least one of a plurality of corresponding detents **37** as recesses in locking protrusion **35** to accommodate engagement of at least one of the cross-brace members **34** therein.

With reference to FIG. 4, there is illustrated a cross-sectional view of the housing **12** illustrating the fluid inlet chamber **22** residing in an upper portion of housing **12** and having the plurality of fluid filtration sub-chambers **31** containing the filter medium **32** therein.

Inlet end cap **14** is also preferably configured as an integral body having the fluid inlet aperture **24** and fluid receiving chamber **26** formed as openings therein. Cap receiving member **14** further consists of an inlet engagement protrusion **25** which projects laterally from the body of end cap **14** and substantially perpendicular to the longitudinal plane thereof. Inlet end cap receiving chamber **24** passes through the inlet engagement projection **25** and is in communication with receiving chamber **26**. Inlet engagement protrusion **25** is configured to correspond in its dimension to fluid inlet chamber **22** such that an interference fit therebetween is achieved upon engagement of end cap **14** with housing **12**. Further, as with outlet end cap **16**, there are also provided at least one of a plurality of locking protrusions **35** and detents **37**, if needed, to provide an interference fit and locking engagement between the end cap **14** and the filtration chamber **30**, or cross-brace members **34** upon engagement of end cap **14** with housing **12** in assembly of the filter unit.

Those skilled in the art will understand and appreciate that filter housing **12** and end caps **14** and **16** may be made of any suitable plastic material, such as polyvinyl-chloride, polycarbonate, or other such plastic material which may be molded or extruded as is known in the

correspond to outlet and inlet caps **14** and **16**, respectively, of the first preferred embodiment of the invention illustrated at water filter **10** in FIGS. 1-5. According to this preferred embodiment of the invention, the inlet receiving end cap has an opening **54** which, when unassembled with housing **42** is in fluid flow communication with inlet chamber **52** to receive a fluid flow therefrom and conduct the fluid flow to the input cap of receiving chamber **56**. Similarly, outlet end cap **46** has an outlet receiving chamber **66** which receives a filtered fluid flow from the filtration chamber **60** and conducts it to an output opening **68** for dispensing. According to this preferred embodiment of filter **40**, a filter member **58** and, if required, a filter retaining member **59** are provided and configured to fit within the chamber defined by locking protrusions **65** on each of the end caps **44** and **46**, such that an interference fit is achieved therebetween. Additionally, filtration chamber **60** is not subdivided, but form a single longitudinal chamber between end caps **44** and **46**.

As with the previously described embodiment **10**, this apparatus according to the second embodiment is made of a suitable plastic material having physical properties of rigidity and malleability sufficient to permit formation of the housing and end caps by extrusion or molding. The filter member **58** is preferably made of a micro-porous polyethylene material such as that marketed under the mark POREX.

While the invention has been described and disclosed with reference to the preferred embodiments thereof, those skilled in the art will understand and appreciate that numerous variations in the basic design or substitution of materials, may be made, but still fall within the intended scope of the invention, which is to be limited only by the claims appended hereto.

7

I claim:

1. A water filtration apparatus, comprising:

an elongated housing defining at least one fluid inlet chamber and at least one fluid filtration chamber therein, said fluid inlet chamber being positioned above and substantially parallel to said fluid filtration chamber, and housing further comprising a fluid inlet aperture in fluid flow communication with said fluid inlet chamber and first and second open ends of said elongated housing;

an inlet cap member having a fluid inlet channel and a fluid receiving chamber defined therein, said inlet cap member being operably coupled to said first open end of said elongated housing, wherein said fluid inlet channel is in fluid flow communication with said fluid inlet chamber of said housing and said fluid receiving chamber is in fluid flow communication with said fluid filtration chamber of said housing;

an outlet cap member having a fluid outlet chamber and a fluid outlet channel defined therein, said outlet cap member being operably coupled to said second open end of said elongated housing, wherein said fluid outlet chamber is in fluid communication with a second end of said fluid filtration chamber and said fluid outlet channel conducts filtered fluid external to said housing; and

at least one filter medium provided in said fluid filtration chamber.

2. The water filtration apparatus according to claim 1, wherein said housing further comprises a generally tubular member having a generally quadrilateral cross-section.

8

ing a communicated fluid flow from said fluid filtration chamber in said housing, said receiving means also providing a fluid tight connection between said outlet cap member and said housing.

8. A water filtration apparatus, comprising:

an elongated housing defining a fluid inlet chamber and a fluid filtration chamber therein, and having first and second open ends thereof, said fluid inlet chamber being positioned above said fluid filtration chamber, said housing further comprising a fluid inlet aperture in fluid flow communication with said fluid inlet chamber and said fluid filtration chamber having disposed therein means for subdividing said fluid filtration chamber into a plurality of horizontally oriented discrete fluid filtration sub-chambers;

an inlet cap member having a fluid inlet channel and a fluid receiving chamber defined therein, said inlet cap member being operably coupled to said first open end of said housing, wherein said fluid inlet channel is in fluid flow communication with said fluid inlet chamber and said fluid receiving chamber is in fluid flow communication with said fluid filtration chamber of said housing;

an outlet cap member having a fluid outlet chamber and a fluid outlet channel defined therein, said outlet cap member being operably coupled to said second open end of said housing, wherein said fluid outlet chamber is in fluid communication with a second end of said fluid filtration chamber and said fluid outlet channel conducts filtered fluid external to said housing;

and at least one filter medium provided in said fluid

3. The water filtration apparatus according to claim 1, wherein said fluid filtration chamber extends an entire lengthwise aspect of said housing and opens at each of said first and said second open ends of said housing.

4. The water filtration apparatus according to claim 1, wherein said fluid inlet chamber extends a substantial lengthwise aspect of said housing.

5. The water filtration apparatus according to claim 2, wherein said generally tubular member further has an arcuate upper section and a quadrilateral lower section, wherein said fluid inlet chamber resides within said arcuate upper section and said fluid filtration chamber resides within said quadrilateral lower section.

6. The water filtration apparatus according to claim 1, wherein said fluid inlet end cap further comprises first communication means for communicating a fluid flow from said fluid inlet chamber in said housing to said fluid inlet channel in said fluid inlet end cap, said first communication means further comprising an engagement protrusion projecting laterally from said inlet cap member, wherein said fluid inlet aperture is formed in said engagement protrusion; and second communication means for communicating a fluid flow from said fluid receiving chamber in said inlet end cap member to said filtration chamber in said housing, said second communication means further comprising at least one locking protrusion projection laterally from said inlet end cap member, wherein said at least one locking protrusion is adjacent to said fluid receiving chamber in said inlet end cap member, wherein said first and second communication means provide a fluid tight connection between said inlet end cap member and said housing.

7. The water filtration apparatus according to claim 1, wherein said fluid outlet chamber of said outlet cap member further comprises receiving means for receiv-

filtration chamber.

9. The water filtration apparatus according to claim 5, further comprising a diverter valve which operably couples to a faucet, fluid conduit connected to said diverter valve, connection means for connecting said fluid conduit to said fluid inlet aperture in said housing and a spigot operably connected to said fluid outlet channel of said outlet cap member.

10. The water filtration apparatus according to claim 9, wherein said connection means further comprises a fluid coupling.

11. The water filtration apparatus according to claim 9, wherein said spigot is rotatable within said fluid outlet channel.

12. The water filtration apparatus according to claim 4, wherein said means for sub-dividing said fluid filtration chamber further comprises at least one cross-brace member provided within said fluid filtration chamber and extending a substantial lengthwise aspect of said fluid filtration chamber.

13. An apparatus for purifying water, comprising:
an elongated housing defining at least one fluid inlet chamber and at least one fluid filtration chamber therein, said at least one inlet chamber and said at least one fluid filtration chamber extending parallel to a longitudinal axis of said housing, wherein said fluid inlet chamber is positioned above and substantially parallel to said fluid filtration chamber, said housing further comprising a fluid inlet aperture in fluid flow communication with said fluid inlet chamber and first and second open ends of said elongated housing;
an inlet end cap having a fluid flow channel and a fluid flow receiving chamber defined therein, said inlet end cap being operably coupled to said first

9

open end of said elongated housing, wherein said fluid flow channel is in fluid flow communication with each of said fluid inlet chamber of said housing and said fluid flow receiving chamber, said fluid flow receiving chamber also being in fluid flow communication with said fluid filtration chamber of said elongated housing, wherein a flow of fluid is received by said fluid flow channel from said fluid inlet chamber and conducted through said fluid flow channel to said fluid flow receiving chamber, and therethrough to said fluid filtration chamber in said elongated housing;

an outlet end cap having a fluid outlet channel defined therein, said outlet cap member being operably coupled to said second open end of said elongated housing, wherein said fluid outlet channel is in fluid communication with a second end of said fluid filtration chamber in said housing, wherein the flow of fluid is received by said fluid outlet channel and conducted external to said elongated housing; and

at least one filter medium provided in said fluid filtration chamber.

14. The apparatus according to claim 13, wherein said housing further comprises a tubular member having a generally quadrilateral cross-section.

15. The apparatus according to claim 14, wherein said generally tubular member further has an arcuate upper section and a quadrilateral lower section, wherein said fluid inlet chamber resides within said arcuate upper section and said fluid filtration chamber resides within said quadrilateral lower section.

16. The apparatus according to claim 13, wherein said

10

an elongated housing defining at least one fluid inlet chamber and at least one fluid filtration chamber therein, said at least one inlet chamber and said at least one fluid filtration chamber extending parallel to a longitudinal axis of said housing, wherein said fluid inlet chamber is positioned above said fluid filtration chamber, said housing further comprising a fluid inlet aperture passing therethrough in fluid flow communication with said fluid inlet chamber, first and second open ends thereof, and said fluid filtration chamber having disposed therein a means for sub-dividing said fluid filtration chamber into a plurality of horizontally oriented discrete fluid filtration sub-chambers;

an inlet end cap having a fluid inlet channel and a fluid flow receiving chamber defined therein, said inlet end cap being operably coupled to said first open end of said elongated housing, wherein said fluid flow channel is in fluid flow communication with said fluid inlet chamber and in fluid flow communication with said fluid flow receiving chamber which is in fluid flow communication with said fluid filtration chamber of said elongated housing, wherein a flow of fluid is received by said fluid flow channel form said fluid inlet chamber and conducted through said fluid flow channel to said fluid flow receiving chamber, and therethrough to said fluid filtration chamber in said elongated housing;

an outlet end cap having a fluid outlet channel defined therein, said outlet cap member being operably coupled to said second open end of said elongated housing, wherein said fluid outlet channel is

fluid inlet chamber substantially extends the entire longitudinal axis of said housing.

17. The apparatus according to claim 13, wherein said fluid filtration chamber extends the entire longitudinal axis of said housing and opens at each of said first and said second open ends of said housing.

18. The apparatus according to claim 13, wherein said inlet end cap further comprises an engagement protrusion projecting laterally from said inlet end cap, wherein said fluid inlet opening is formed in said engagement protrusion; and at least one locking protrusion projecting laterally from said inlet end cap, wherein said at least one locking protrusion is adjacent to said fluid receiving chamber in said inlet end cap, said engagement protrusion and said at least one locking protrusion each, being configured to operably engage and couple one of said first and second open ends of said housing in fluid-tight engagement.

19. The apparatus according to claim 13, wherein said outlet end cap further comprises receiving means for receiving a communicated fluid flow from said fluid filtration chamber in said housing, said receiving means also providing a fluid tight connection between said outlet cap member and said housing.

20. An apparatus for purifying water, comprising:

in fluid flow communication with a second end of said fluid filtration chamber in said housing, wherein the flow of fluid is received by said fluid outlet channel and conducted external to said elongated housing; and

at least one filter medium provided in said fluid filtration chamber.

21. The apparatus according to claim 20, further comprising a diverter valve which operably couples to a faucet, fluid conduit connected to said diverter valve, connection means for connecting said fluid conduit to said fluid inlet aperture in said housing and a spigot operably connected to said fluid outlet channel of said outlet cap member.

22. The apparatus according to claim 21, wherein said connection means further comprises a fluid coupling.

23. The apparatus according to claim 21, wherein said spigot is rotatable within said fluid outlet channel.

24. The apparatus according to claim 20 wherein said means for sub-dividing said fluid filtration chamber further comprises at least one cross-brace member provided within said fluid filtration chamber and extending a substantial lengthwise aspect of said fluid filtration chamber.

* * * * * *

APPENDIX B

United States Patent [19]

Ferguson

[11] Patent Number: **Des. 318,092**

[45] Date of Patent: ∗∗ **Jul. 9, 1991**

[54] **WATER FILTER OR SIMILAR ARTICLE**

[76] Inventor: George Ferguson, 7740 E. Glenrosa, No. 112, Scottsdale, Ariz. 85251

[∗∗] Term: **14 Years**

[21] Appl. No.: 482,404

[22] Filed: Feb. 20, 1990
[52] U.S. Cl. D23/209
[58] Field of Search D23/200, 207–210; 210/136, 198.1, 205–206, 231, 241, 244–245, 257.1–257.2, 258, 260–261, 269, 275, 282, 288–290, 295, 321.6, 321.78, 416.3, 443–449

[56] **References Cited**

U.S. PATENT DOCUMENTS

D. 282,767	7/1986	Shofner	D23/209
D. 296,126	6/1988	Clark	D23/207
D. 296,463	6/1988	Padillo	D23/207 X
D. 307,933	5/1990	Baer	D23/209
D. 310,707	9/1990	Sedman	D23/209
4,218,317	8/1980	Nirschmann	210/449 X

Primary Examiner—Susan J. Lucas
Assistant Examiner—M. H. Tung
Attorney, Agent, or Firm—David G. Rosenbaum

[57] **CLAIM**

The ornamental design for a water filter, as shown and described.

DESCRIPTION

FIG. 1 is a front perspective view of a water filter showing my new design, on an enlarged scale;
FIG. 2 is an end elevational view thereof;
FIG. 3 is a rear elevational view thereof.
FIG. 4 is a bottom plan view thereof.
The ends of the filter are shaded to indicate a contrast.

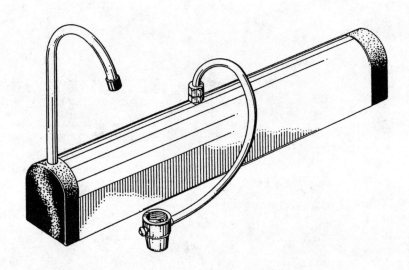

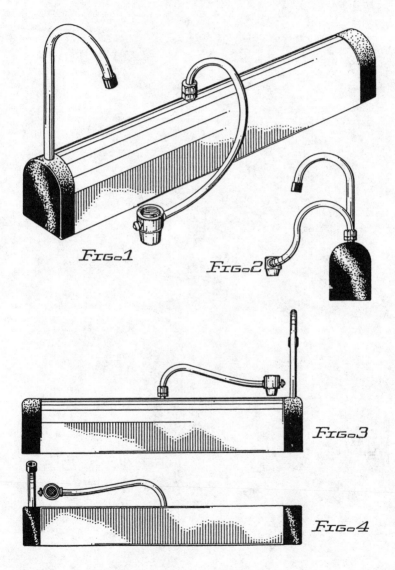

Fig.1

Fig.2

Fig.3

Fig.4

APPENDIX C

Reference Collections of U.S. Patents and Trademarks
Available for Public Use in Patent and Trademark Depository Libraries

The following libraries, designated as Patent and Trademark Depository Libraries (PTDLs), receive patent and trademark information in various formats from the U.S. Patent and Trademark Office. Many PTDLs have on file all full-text patents issued since 1790, trademarks published since 1872, and select collections of foreign patents. All PDTLs have both the patent and trademark sections of the *Official Gazette of the U. S. Patent and Trademark Office*. The full-text utility and design patents are distributed numerically on 16 mm microfilm, and plant patents on color microfiche. Patent and trademark search systems on CD-ROM (Compact Disc-Read Only) format are available at all PTDLs to increase utilization of and enhance access to the information found in patents and trademarks. It is through the CD-ROM systems that preliminary patent and trademark searches can be conducted through the numerically arranged collections.

All information is available for use by the public free of char

In addition, each PTDL offers reference publications wh outline and provide access to the patent and trademark class cation systems, as well as other documents and publicati which supplement the basic search tools. PTDLs provide te nical staff assistance in using all materials. Facilities for making paper copies of patent and trademark information are generally provided for a fee.

Since there are variations in the scope of patent and trademark collections among the PTDLs, and their hours of service to the public vary, anyone contemplating use of these collections at a particular library is urged to contact that library in advance about its collections, services, and hours in order to avert possible inconvenience.

State	Name of Library	Telephone Contact
Alabama	Auburn University Libraries	(205) 844-1747
	Birmingham Public Library	(205) 226-3680
Alaska	Anchorage: Z. J. Loussac Public Library	(907) 562-7323
Arizona	Tempe: Noble Library, Arizona State University	(602) 965-7010
Arkansas	Little Rock: Arkansas State Library	(501) 682-2053
California	Los Angeles Public Library	(213) 612-3273
	Sacramento: California State Library	(916) 654-0069
	San Diego Public Library	(619) 236-5813
	Sunnyvale Patent Clearinghouse	(408) 730-7290
Colorado	Denver Public Library	(303) 640-8847
Connecticut	New Haven: Science Park Library	(203) 786-5447
Delaware	Newark: University of Delaware Library	(302) 831-2965
Dist. of Columbia	Washington: Howard University Libraries	(202) 806-7252
Florida	Fort Lauderdale: Broward County Main Library	(305) 357-7444
	Miami-Dade Public Library	(305) 375-2665
	Orlando: University of Central Florida Libraries	(407) 823-2562
	Tampa: Tampa Campus Library, University of South Florida	(813) 974-2726

Georgia	Atlanta: Price Gilbert Memorial Library, Georgia Institute of Technology	(404) 894-4508
Hawaii	Honolulu: Hawaii State Public Library System	(808) 586-3477
Idaho	Moscow: University of Idaho Library	(208) 885-6235
Illinois	Chicago Public Library	(312) 747-4450
	Springfield: Illinois State Library	(217) 782-5659
Indiana	Indianapolis-Marion County Public Library	(317) 269-1741
	West Lafayette: Siegesmund Engineering Library, Purdue University	(317) 494-2873
Iowa	Des Moines: State Library of Iowa	(515) 281-4118
Kansas	Wichita: Ablah Library, Wichita State University	(316) 689-3155
Kentucky	Louisville Free Public Library	(502) 561-8617
Louisiana	Baton Rouge: Troy H. Middleton Library, Louisiana State University	(504) 388-2570
Maryland	College Park: Engineering and Physical Sciences Library, University of Maryland	(301) 405-9157
Massachusetts	Amherst: Physical Sciences Library, University of Massachusetts	(413) 545-1370
	Boston Public Library	(617) 536-5400 Ext. 265
Michigan	Ann Arbor: Engineering Library, University of Michigan	(313) 764-5298
	Big Rapids: Abigail S. Timme Library, Ferris State University	(616) 592-3602
	Detroit Public Library	(313) 833-1450
Minnesota	Minneapolis Public Library and Information Center	(612) 372-6570
Mississippi	Jackson: Mississippi Library Commission	Not Yet Operational
Missouri	Kansas City: Linda Hall Library	(816) 363-4600
	St. Louis Public Library	(314) 241-2288 Ext. 390
Montana	Butte: Montana College of Mineral Science and Technology Library	(406) 496-4281
Nebraska	Lincoln: Engineering Library, University of Nebraska-Lincoln	(402) 472-3411
Nevada	Reno: University of Nevada, Reno Library	(702) 784-6579
New Hampshire	Durham: University of New Hampshire Library	(603) 862-1777
New Jersey	Newark Public Library	(201) 733-7782
	Piscataway: Library of Science and Medicine, Rutgers University	(908) 932-2895
New Mexico	Albuquerque: University of New Mexico General Library	(505) 277-4412
New York	Albany: New York State Library	(518) 473-4636
	Buffalo and Erie County Public Library	(716) 858-7101
	New York Public Library (The Research Libraries)	(212) 930-8574
North Carolina	Raleigh: D.H. Hill Library, North Carolina State University	(919) 515-3280

Reference Collections of U. S. Patents and Trademarks Available for Public Use in Patent and Trademark
Depository Libraries—(continued)

State	Name of Library	Telephone Contact
North Dakota	Grand Forks: Chester Fritz Library, University of North Dakota	(701) 777-4888
Ohio	Cincinnati and Hamilton County, Public Library of	(513) 369-6936
	Cleveland Public Library	(216) 623-2870
	Columbus: Ohio State University Libraries	(614) 292-6175
	Toledo/Lucas County Public Library	(419) 259-5212
Oklahoma	Stillwater: Oklahoma State University Center for International Trade	
	Development	(405) 744-7086
Oregon	Salem: Oregon State Library	(503) 378-4239
Pennsylvania	Philadelphia, The Free Library of	(215) 686-5331
	Pittsburgh, Carnegie Library of	(412) 622-3138
	University Park: Pattee Library, Pennsylvania State University	(814) 865-4861
Rhode Island	Providence Public Library	(401) 455-8027
South Carolina	Charleston: Medical University of South Carolina Library	(803) 792-2372
	Clemson University Libraries	Not Yet Operational
Tennessee	Memphis & Shelby County Public Library and Information Center	(901) 725-8877
	Nashville: Stevenson Science Library, Vanderbilt University	(615) 322-2775
Texas	Austin: McKinney Engineering Library, University of Texas at Austin	(512) 495-4500
	College Station: Sterling C. Evans Library, Texas A & M University	(409) 845-3826
	Dallas Public Library	(214) 670-1468
	Houston: The Fondren Library, Rice University	(713) 527-8101 Ext.2587
Utah	Salt Lake City: Marriott Library, University of Utah	(801) 581-8394
Virginia	Richmond: James Branch Cabell Library, Virginia Commonwealth University	(804) 367-1104
Washington	Seattle: Engineering Library, University of Washington	(206) 543-0740
West Virginia	Morgantown: Evansdale Library, West Virginia University	(304) 293-2510
Wisconsin	Madison: Kurt F. Wendt Library, University of Wisconsin Madison	(608) 262-6845
	Milwaukee Public Library	(414) 278-3247

APPENDIX D

U. S. PATENT AND TRADEMARK OFFICE
Effective October 1, 1992

The U. S. Patent and Trademark Office has amended its rules of practice in patent and trademark cases, Parts 1 and 2 of Title 37, Code of Federal Regulations to adjust patent and trademark fee amounts.

Any fee payment due and paid on or after October 1, 1992, must be paid in the revised amount. The date of mailing indicated on a proper Certificate of Mailing under either 37 CFR 1.8 or 37 CFR 1.10 will be considered to be the date of receipt and payment in the Office.

As this fee sheet is a summary and the content of rules also may be changing, you should refer to the notice published in the Federal Register on August 21, 1992 at 57 FR Part VI. See also the Official Gazette of the United States Patent and Trademark Office of August 25, 1992.

The fees which are subject to reduction for small entities who have established status (37 CFR 1.27) are shown in a separate column.

Fee Code	37 CFR	Description	Fee	Small Entity Fee If applicable
		PATENT FEES		
Filing Fees				
101 / 201	1.16(a)	Basic filing fee - utility	710.00	355.00
102 / 202	1.16(b)	Independent claims in excess of three	74.00	37.00
103 / 203	1.16(c)	Claims in excess of twenty	22.00	11.00
104 / 204	1.16(d)	Multiple dependent claim	230.00	115.00
105 / 205	1.16(e)	Surcharge- Late filing fee or oath or declaration.	130.00	65.00
106 / 206	1.16(f)	Design filing fee	290.00	145.00
107 / 207	1.16(g)	Plant filing fee	480.00	240.00
108 / 208	1.16(h)	Reissue filing fee	710.00	355.00
109 / 209	1.16(i)	Reissue independent claims over original patent	74.00	37.00
110 / 210	1.16(j)	Reissue claims in excess of 20 and over original patent	22.00	11.00
139	1.17(k)	Non-English specification	130.00	
Extension Fees				
115 / 215	1.17(a)	Extension for response within first month	110.00	55.00
116 / 216	1.17(b)	Extension for response within second month	360.00	180.00
117 / 217	1.17(c)	Extension for response within third month	840.00	420.00
118 / 218	1.17(d)	Extension for response within fourth month	1,320.00	660.00
Appeals/Interference Fees				
119 / 219	1.17(e)	Notice of appeal	270.00	135.00
120 / 220	1.17(f)	Filing a brief in support of an appeal	270.00	135.00
121 / 221	1.17(g)	Request for oral hearing	230.00	115.00
Issue Fees				
142 / 242	1.18(a)	Utility issue fee	1,170.00	585.00
143 / 243	1.18(b)	Design issue fee	410.00	205.00
144 / 244	1.18(c)	Plant issue fee	590.00	295.00
Miscellaneous Fees				
111	1.20(j)	Extension of term of patent	1000.00	
112	1.17(n)	Requesting publication of SIR - Prior to examiner's action	820.00*	
113	1.17(o)	Requesting publication of SIR - After examiner's action	1,640.00*	
145	1.20(a)	Certificate of correction	100.00	
147	1.20(c)	For filing a request for reexamination	2,250.00	
148 / 248	1.20(d)	Statutory Disclaimer	110.00	55.00

Reduced by Basic Filing Fee Paid

Fee Code	37 CFR	Description	Fee	Small Entity Fee if applicable

Patent Petition Fees

Fee Code	37 CFR	Description	Fee	Small Entity Fee if applicable
122		Petitions to the Commissioner, unless otherwise specified	130.00	
126	1.17(p)	Submission of an Information Disclosure Statement (§1.97(c))	200.00	
138	1.17(j)	Petition to institute a public use proceeding	1,350.00	
140 / 240	1.17(l)	Petition to revive unavoidably abandoned application	110.00 /	55.00
141 / 241	1.17(m)	Petition to revive unintentionally abandoned application	1,170.00 /	585.00

Maintenance Fees : **Applications Filed on or after December 12, 1980**

Fee Code	37 CFR	Description	Fee	Small Entity Fee if applicable
183 / 283	1.20(e)	Due at 3.5 years	930.00 /	465.00
184 / 284	1.20(f)	Due at 7.5 years	1,870.00 /	935.00
185 / 285	1.20(g)	Due at 11.5 years	2,820.00 /	1,410.00
186 / 286	1.20(h)	Surcharge - Late payment within 6 months.	130.00 /	65.00
187	1.20(i)	Surcharge after expiration	620.00	

PCT Fees - National Stage

Fee Code	37 CFR	Description	Fee	Small Entity Fee if applicable
154 / 254	1.492(e)	Surcharge - Late filing fee or oath or declaration	130.00 /	65.00
156	1.492(f)	English translation - after twenty months	130.00	
956 / 957	1.492(a)(1)	IPEA - U.S.	640.00 /	320.00
958 / 959	1.492(a)(2)	ISA - U.S.	710.00 /	355.00
960 / 961	1.492(a)(3)	PTO not ISA or IPEA	950.00 /	475.00
962 / 963	1.492(a)(4)	Claims meet PCT Article 33(1)-(4) - IPEA - U.S.	90.00 /	45.00
964 / 965	1.492(b)	Claims - extra independent (over three)	74.00 /	37.00
966 / 967	1.492(c)	Claims - extra total (over twenty)	22.00 /	11.00
968 / 969	1.492(d)	Claims - multiple dependent	230.00 /	115.00
970 / 971	1.492(a)(5)	For filing with EPO or JPO search report	830.00 /	415.00

PCT Fees - International Stage

Fee Code	37 CFR	Description	Fee	Small Entity Fee if applicable
150	1.445(a)(1)	Transmittal fee	200.00	
151	1.445(a)(2)	PCT search fee - no U.S. application	620.00	
152	1.445 (a)(3)	Supplemental search per additional invention	170.00	
153	1.445(a)(2)	PCT search- prior U.S. application	410.00	
190	1.482(a)(1)	Preliminary examination fee - ISA was the U.S.	450.00	
191	1.482(a)(1)	Preliminary examination fee - ISA not the U.S.	670.00	
192	1.482(a)(2)	Additional invention - ISA was the U.S.	140.00	
193	1.482(a)(2)	Additional invention - ISA not the U.S.	230.00	

PCT Fees to WIPO

Fee Code	37 CFR	Description	Fee	Small Entity Fee if applicable
800		Basic fee (first thirty pages)	525.00*	
801		Basic supplemental fee (for each page over thirty)	10.00*	
803		Handling fee	161.00*	
805 - 898		Designation fee per country	127.00*	

PCT Fee to EPO

Fee Code	37 CFR	Description	Fee	Small Entity Fee if applicable
802		International search	1,635.00*	

*WIPO and EPO fees subject to periodic change due to fluctuations in exchange rate. Refer to Patent Official Gazette for current amounts.

85

Fee Code	37 CFR	Description	Fee

TRADEMARK FEES

Trademark Processing Fees

Fee Code	37 CFR	Description	Fee
361	2.6(a)(1)	Application for registration, per class	210.00
362	2.6(a)(2)	Filing an Amendment to Allege Use under § 1(c), per class	100.00
363	2.6(a)(3)	Filing a Statement of Use under § 1(d)(1), per class	100.00
364	2.6(a)(4)	Filing a Request for a Six-month Extension of Time for Filing a Statement of Use under § 1(d)(1), per class	100.00
365	2.6(a)(5)	Application for renewal, per class	300.00
366	2.6(a)(6)	Additional fee for late renewal, per class	100.00
367	2.6(a)(7)	Publication of mark under §12(c), per class	100.00
368	2.6(a)(8)	Issuing new certificate of registration	100.00
369	2.6(a)(9)	Certificate of Correction, registrant's error	100.00
370	2.6(a)(10)	Filing disclaimer to registration	100.00
371	2.6(a)(11)	Filing amendment to registration	100.00
372	2.6(a)(12)	Filing § 8 affidavit, per class	100.00
373	2.6(a)(13)	Filing § 15 affidavit, per class	100.00
374	2.6(a)(14)	Filing combined §§ 8 & 15 affidavit, per class	200.00
375	2.6(a)(15)	Petition to the Commissioner	100.00
376	2.6(a)(16)	Petition for cancellation, per class	200.00
377	2.6(a)(17)	Notice of opposition, per class	200.00
378	2.6(a)(18)	Ex parte appeal, per class	100.00
379	2.6(a)(19)	Dividing an application, per new application (file wrapper) created	100.00

Trademark Service Fees

Fee Code	37 CFR	Description	Fee
461	2.6(b)(1)(i)	Printed copy of each registered mark, regular service	3.00
462	2.6(b)(1)(ii)	Printed copy of each registered mark, expedited local service	6.00
463	2.6(b)(1)(iii)	Printed copy of each registered mark ordered via EOS, expedited service	25.00
464	2.6(b)(4)(i)	Certified copy of registered mark, with title and/or status, regular service	10.00
465	2.6(b)(4)(ii)	Certified copy of registered mark, with title and/or status, expedited local service	20.00
466	2.6(b)(2)(i)	Certified or uncertified copy of trademark application as filed, regular service	12.00
467	2.6(b)(2)(ii)	Certified or uncertified copy of trademark application as filed, expedited local service	24.00
468	2.6(b)(3)	Certified or uncertified copy of trademark-related file wrapper and contents	50.00
469	2.6(b)(5)	Certified or uncertified copy of trademark document, unless otherwise provided	25.00
470	2.6(b)(7)	For assignment records, abstracts of title and certification per registration	25.00
475	1.19(g)	Comparing and certifying copies, per document, per copy	25.00
480	2.6(b)(9)	Self-service copy charge, per page	0.25
481	2.6(b)(6)	Recording trademark assignment, agreement or other paper, first mark per document	40.00
482		For second and subsequent marks in the same document	25.00
484	2.6(b)(10)	Labor charges for services, per hour or fraction thereof	30.00
485	2.6(b)(11)	Unspecified other services	AT COST
488	2.6(b)(8)	Each hour of T-SEARCH terminal session time	40.00
490	1.24	Trademark coupons	3.00

GENERAL FEES

Finance Service Fees

Fee Code	37 CFR	Description	Fee
607	1.21(b-1)	Establish deposit account	10.00
608	1.21(b)(2)	Service charge for below minimum balance	25.00
608	1.21(b)(3)	Service charge for below minimum balance restricted subscription deposit account	25.00
617	1.21(m)	Processing returned checks	50.00

Computer Service Fees

Fee Code	37 CFR	Description	Fee
618		Computer records	AT COST

Fee Code	37 CFR	Description	Fee

Patent Service Fees

Fee Code	37 CFR	Description	Fee
561	1.19(a)(1)(i)	Printed copy of patent w/o color, regular service	3.00
562	1.19(a)(1)(ii)	Printed copy of patent w/o color, expedited local service	6.00
563	1.19(a)(1)(iii)	Printed copy of patent w/o color, ordered via EOS, expedited service	25.00
564	1.19(a)(2)	Printed copy of plant patent, in color	12.00
565	1.19(a)(3)	Copy of utility patent or SIR, with color drawings	24.00
566	1.19(b)(1)(i)	Certified or uncertified copy of patent application as filed, regular service	12.00
567	1.19(b)(1)(ii)	Certified or uncertified copy of patent application, expedited local service	24.00
568	1.19(b)(2)	Certified or uncertified copy of patent-related file wrapper and contents	150.00
569	1.19(b)(3)	Certified or uncertified copy of document, unless otherwise provided	25.00
570	1.19(b)(4)	For assignment records, abstract of title and certification, per patent	25.00
571	1.19(c)	Library Service	50.00
572	1.19(d)	List of U.S. patents and SIRs in subclass	3.00
573	1.19(e)	Uncertified statement re status of maintenance fee payments	10.00
574	1.19(f)	Copy of non-U.S. document	25.00
575	1.19(g)	Comparing and Certifying Copies, Per Document, Per Copy	25.00
576	1.19(h)	Additional filing receipt, duplicate or corrected due to applicant error	25.00
577	1.21(c)	Filing a Disclosure Document	10.00
578	1.21(d)	Local delivery box rental, per annum	50.00
579	1.21(e)	International type search report	40.00
580	1.21(g)	Self-service copy charge, per page	0.25
581	1.21(h)	Recording each patent assignment, agreement or other paper, per property	40.00
583	1.21(i)	Publication in Official Gazette	25.00
584	1.21(j)	Labor charges for services, per hour or fraction thereof	30.00
585	1.21(k)	Unspecified other services	AT COST
586	1.21(l)	Retaining abandoned application	130.00
587	1.21(n)	Handling fee for incomplete or improper application	130.00
588	1.21(o)	Automated Patent System (APS- Text) terminal session time, per hr.	40.00
590	1.24	Patent coupons	3.00
591	1.21(p)	APS-Text terminal session time, per hr., at the PTDLs	70.00*
589	1.296	Handling fee for withdrawal of SIR	130.00

Patent Enrollment Fees

Fee Code	37 CFR	Description	Fee
609	1.21(a)(1)	Admission to examination	300.00
610	1.21(a)(2)	Registration to practice	100.00
611	1.21(a)(3)	Reinstatement to practice	15.00
612	1.21(a)(4)	Copy of certificate of good standing	10.00
613	1.21(a)(4)	Certificate of good standing - suitable for framing	20.00
615	1.21(a)(5)	Review of decision of Director, Office of Enrollment and Discipline	130.00
616	1.21(a)(6)	Regrading of Examination	130.00

* Collection of the fee for APS-Text access at the PTDLs has been suspended until further notice.

APPENDIX E

DECLARATION FOR PATENT APPLICATION

Docket No. _____

As a below named inventor, I hereby declare that:

My residence, post office address and citizenship are as stated below next to my name.

I believe I am the original, first and sole inventor (if only one name is listed below) or an original, first and joint inventor (if plural names are listed below) of the subject matter which is claimed and for which a patent is sought on the invention entitled _____, the specification of which

(check one) ☐ is attached hereto.
             ☐ was filed on _____ as
             Application Serial No. _____
             and was amended on _____ (if applicable).

I hereby state that I have reviewed and understand the contents of the above identified specification, including the claims, as amended by any amendment referred to above.

I acknowledge the duty to disclose information which is material to the examination of this application in accordance with Title 37, Code of Federal Regulations, §1.56(a).

I hereby claim foreign priority benefits under Title 35, United States Code, §119 of any foreign application(s) for patent or inventor's certificate listed below and have also identified below any foreign application for patent or inventor's certificate having a filing date before that of the application on which priority is claimed:

Prior Foreign Application(s)   Priority Claimed

(Number)	(Country)	(Day/Month/Year Filed)	Yes	No
(Number)	(Country)	(Day/Month/Year Filed)	Yes	No
(Number)	(Country)	(Day/Month/Year Filed)	Yes	No

I hereby claim the benefit under Title 35, United States Code, §120 of any United States application(s) listed below and, insofar as the subject matter of each of the claims of this application is not disclosed in the prior United States application in the manner provided by the first paragraph of Title 35, United States Code, §112, I acknowledge the duty to disclose material information as defined in Title 37, Code of Federal Regulations, §1.56(a) which occurred between the filing date of the prior application and the national or PCT international filing date of this application:

(Application Serial No.)	(Filing Date)	(Status—patented, pending, abandoned)
(Application Serial No.)	(Filing Date)	(Status—patented, pending, abandoned)

I hereby appoint the following attorney(s) and/or agent(s) to prosecute this application and to transact all business in the Patent and Trademark Office connected therewith:

_____.

Address all telephone calls to _____ at telephone no. _____.
Address all correspondence to _____
_____
_____
_____

I hereby declare that all statements made herein of my own knowledge are true and that all statements made on information and belief are believed to be true; and further that these statements were made with the knowledge that willful false statements and the like so made are punishable by fine or imprisonment, or both, under Section 1001 of Title 18 of the United States Code and that such willful false statements may jeopardize the validity of the application or any patent issued thereon.

Full name of sole or first inventor _____
Inventor's signature _____ Date _____
Residence _____ Citizenship _____
Post Office Address _____

Full name of second joint inventor, if any _____ –
Second Inventor's signature _____ Date _____
Residence _____ Citizenship _____
Post Office Address _____

(Supply similar information and signature for third and subsequent joint inventors.)

Form PTO-FB-A110 (8-83)

89

APPENDIX F

Applicant or Patentee:_____ Attorney's
Serial or Patent No.:_____ Docket No.:_____
Filed or Issued:_____
For:_____

VERIFIED STATEMENT (DECLARATION) CLAIMING SMALL ENTITY STATUS
(37 CFR 1.9(f) & 1.27(c)) - INDEPENDENT INVENTOR

As a below named inventor, I hereby declare that I qualify as an independent inventor as defined in 37 CFR 1.9(c) for purposes of paying reduced fees under section 41(a) and (b) of Title 35, United States Code, to the Patent and Trademark Office with regard to the invention entitled _____
described in

    [ ] the specification filed herewith
    [ ] application serial number _____, filed _____
    [ ] patent number _____, issued _____

I have not assigned, granted, conveyed or licensed and am under no obligation under contract or law to assign, grant, convey or license, any rights to the invention to any person who could not be classified as an independent inventor under 37 CFR 1.9(c) if that person made the invention, or to any concern which would not qualify as a small business concern under 37 CFR 1.9(d) or a nonprofit organization under 37 CFR 1.9(a).

Each person, concern or organization to which I have assigned, granted, conveyed, or licensed or am under an obligation under contract or law to assign, grant, convey, or license any rights in the invention is listed below:

    [ ] No such person, concern, or organization
    [ ] Persons, concerns or organizations listed below*

    * Note: Separate verified statements are required from each named person, concern or organization having rights to the invention averring to their status as small entities. (37 CFR 1.27)

NAME _____
ADDRESS _____
    [ ] INDIVIDUAL   [ ] SMALL BUSINESS CONCERN   [ ] NONPROFIT ORGANIZATION

NAME _____
ADDRESS _____
    [ ] INDIVIDUAL   [ ] SMALL BUSINESS CONCERN   [ ] NONPROFIT ORGANIZATION

NAME _____
ADDRESS _____
    [ ] INDIVIDUAL   [ ] SMALL BUSINESS CONCERN   [ ] NONPROFIT ORGANIZATION

    I acknowledge the duty To file, in this application or patent, notification of any change in status resulting in loss of entitlement to small entity status prior to paying, or at the time of paying, the earliest of the issue fee or any maintenance fee due after the date an which status as a small entity is no longer appropriate. (37 CFR 1.28(b))

    I hereby declare that all statements made herein of my own knowledge are true and that all statements made on information and belief are believed to be true; and further that these statements were made with the knowledge that willful false statements and the like so made are punishable by fine or imprisonment, or both, under section 1001 of Title 18 of the United States Code, and that such willful false statements may jeopardize the validity of the application, any patent issuing thereon, or any patent to which this verified statement is directed.

_____ _____ _____
NAME OF INVENTOR   NAME OF INVENTOR   NAME OF INVENTOR

_____ _____ _____
Signature of inventor   Signature of inventor   Signature of inventor

_____   _____   _____
Date   Date   Date

Rev. 11, Apr. 1989

APPENDIX G

OMB No. 0651-0011 (12/31/86)

PATENT APPLICATION TRANSMITTAL LETTER	ATTORNEY'S DOCKET NO.

TO THE COMMISSIONER OF PATENTS AND TRADEMARKS:

Transmitted herewith for filing is the patent application of _____

_____

for _____

_____

Enclosed are:

☐ _____ sheets of drawing.

☐ an assignment of the invention to _____

_____

☐ a certified copy of a _____ application.

☐ associate power of attorney.

☐ verified statement to establish small entity status under 37 CFR 1.9 and 1.27. ———

CLAIMS AS FILED			SMALL ENTITY			OTHER THAN A SMALL ENTITY	
FOR	NO. FILED	NO. EXTRA	RATE	FEE	_OR_	RATE	FEE
BASIC FEE				$	_OR_		$
TOTAL CLAIMS	- 20 -	*	x $6 =	$	_OR_	x $ 1 2 =	$
INDEP CLAIMS	- 3 -	*	x $17=	$	_OR_	x $34 =	$
MULTIPLE DEPENDENT CLAIM PRESENT			+ $ 65 =	$	_OR_	+ $ 11 0 =	$
* If the difference in col. 1 is less than zero, enter "0" in col. 2			TOTAL	$	_OR_	TOTAL	$

☐ Please charge my Deposit Account No. _____ in the amount of $ _____
☐ A duplicate copy of this sheet is enclosed.

☐ A check in the amount of $ _____ to cover the filing fee is enclosed.

☐ The Commissioner is hereby authorized to charge payment of the following fees associated with this communication or credit any overpayment to Deposit Account No. _____ . A Duplicate copy of this sheet is enclosed.

    ☐ Any additional filing fees required under 37 CFR 1.16.

    ☐ Any patent application processing fees under 37 CFR 1.17

☐ The Commissioner is hereby authorized to charge payment of the following fees during the pendency of this application or credit any overpayment to Deposit Account No. _____ . A duplicate copy of this sheet is enclosed.

    ☐ Any filing fees under 37 CFR 1.16 for presentation of extra claims.

    ☐ Any patent application processing fees under 37 CFR 1.17.

    ☐ The issue fee set in 37 CFR 1.18 at or before mailing of the Notice of Allowance, pursuant to 37 CFR 1.311(b).

_____   _____
date   signature

Patent and Trademark Office - U.S. DEPARTMENT of COMMERCE

Form PTO-FB-A510 (10-85)
(also form PTO-1082)

APPENDIX H

INFORMATION DISCLOSURE CITATION	ATTY. DOCKET NO.		SERIAL NO.	
(Use several sheets if necessary)	APPLICANT			
	FILING DATE		GROUP	

U.S. PATENT DOCUMENTS

*EXAMINER INITIAL	DOCUMENT NUMBER	DATE	NAME	CLASS	SUBCLASS	FILING DATE IF APPROPRIATE

FOREIGN PATENT DOCUMENTS

	DOCUMENT NUMBER	DATE	COUNTRY	CLASS	SUBCLASS	TRANSLATION YES	NO

OTHER DOCUMENTS (Including Author, Title, Date, Pertinent Pages, Etc.)

EXAMINER	DATE CONSIDERED

*EXAMINER: Initial if reference considered, whether or not citation is in conformance with MPEP 609; Draw line through citation if not in conformance and not considered. Include copy of this form with next communication to applicant.

Form PTO-FB-A820
(also form PTO-1449)

Patent and Trademark Office - U.S. DEPARTMENT of COMMERCE

92

APPENDIX I

U.S. PATENT PROSECUTION

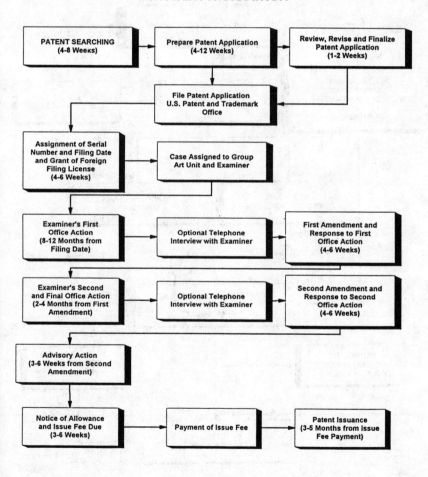

APPENDIX J

U.S. PATENT AND COURT SYSTEM

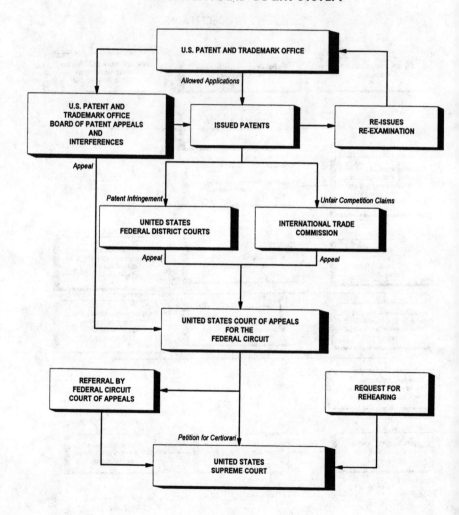

APPENDIX K

TRADEMARK/SERVICE MARK APPLICATION, PRINCIPAL REGISTER, WITH DECLARATION	MARK (Identify the mark:)
	CLASS NO (If known)

TO THE ASSISTANT SECRETARY AND COMMISSIONER OF PATENTS AND TRADEMARKS:

APPLICANT NAME

APPLICANT BUSINESS ADDRESS

APPLICANT ENTITY (Check one and supply requested information)

☐ Individual - Citizenship: (Country) _____

☐ Partnership - Partnership Domicile: (State and Country) _____
Names and Citizenship (Country) of General Partners: _____

☐ Corporation - State (Country, if appropriate) of Incorporation: _____

☐ Other: (Specify Nature of Entity and Domicile) _____

GOODS AND/OR SERVICES:

Applicant requests registration of the above-identified trademark/service mark shown in the accompanying drawing in the United States Patent and Trademark Office on the Principal Register established by the Act of July 5, 1946 (15 U.S.C. 1051 et. seq., as amended.) for the following goods/services: _____

BASIS FOR APPLICATION (Check one or more, but NOT both the first AND second boxes, and supply requested information)

☐ Applicant is using the mark in commerce on or in connection with the above identified goods/services. (15 U.S.C. 1051(a), as amended.) Three specimens showing the mark as used in commerce are submitted with this application.
* Date of first use of the mark anywhere: _____
* Date of first use of the mark in commerce which the U.S. Congress may regulate: _____
* Specify the type of commerce: _____
(e.g., interstate, between the U.S. and a specified foreign country)
* Specify manner or mode of use of mark on or in connection with the goods/services: _____
(e.g., trademark is applied to labels, service mark is used in advertisements)

☐ Applicant has a bona fide intention to use the mark in commerce on or in connection with the above identified goods/services. (15 U.S.C. 1051(b), as amended.)
* Specify intended manner or mode of use of mark on or in connection with the goods/services: _____
(e.g., trademark will be applied to labels, service mark will be used in advertisements)

☐ Applicant has a bona fide intention to use the mark in commerce on or in connection with the above identified goods/services, and asserts a claim of priority based upon a foreign application in accordance with 15 U.S.C. 1126(d), as amended.
* Country of foreign filing: _____ * Date of foreign filing: _____

☐ Applicant has a bona fide intention to use the mark in commerce on or in connection with the above identified goods/services and, accompanying this application, submits a certification or certified copy of a foreign registration in accordance with 15 U.S.C. 1126(e), as amended.
* Country of registration: _____ * Registration number: _____

Note: Declaration, on Reverse Side, MUST be Signed

PTO Form 1478 (REV. 9/89)
OMB No 0651000B
Exp. 5-31-91

U.S. DEPARTMENT OF COMMERCE/Patent and Trademark Office

DECLARATION

The undersigned being hereby warned that willful false statements and the like so made are punishable by fine or imprisonment, or both, under 18 U.S.C. 1001, and that such willful false statements may jeopardize the validity of the application or any resulting registration, declares that he/she is properly authorized to execute this application on behalf of the applicant; he/she believes the applicant to be the owner of the trademark/service mark sought to be registered, or, if the application is being filed under 15 U.S.C. 1051(b), he/she believes applicant to be entitled to use such mark in commerce; to the best of his/her knowledge and belief no other person, firm, corporation, or association has the right to use the above identified mark in commerce, either in the identical form thereof or in such near resemblance thereto as to be likely, when used on or in connection with the goods/services of such other person, to cause confusion, or to cause mistake, or to deceive; and that all statements made of his/her own knowledge are true and all statements made on information and belief are believed to be true.

_____   _____
Date   Signature

_____   _____
Telephone Number   Print or Type Name and Position

INSTRUCTIONS AND INFORMATION FOR APPLICANT

To receive a filing date, the application must be completed and signed by the applicant and submitted along with:

1. The prescribed fee for each class of goods/services listed in the application;
2. A drawing of the mark in conformance with 37 CFR 2.52;
3. If the application is based on use of the mark in commerce, three (3) specimens (evidence) of the mark as used in commerce for each class of goods/services listed in the application. All three specimens may be the same and may be in the nature of: (a) labels showing the mark which are placed on the goods; (b) a photograph of the mark as it appears on the goods, (c) brochures or advertisements showing the mark as used in connection with the services.

Verification of the application - The application must be signed in order for the application to receive a filing date. Only the following person may sign the verification (Declaration) for the application, depending on the applicant's legal entity: (1) the individual applicant; (2) an officer of the corporate applicant; (c) one general partner of a partnership applicant; (d) all joint applicants.

Additional information concerning the requirements for filing an application are available in a booklet entitled **Basic Facts about Trademarks**, which may be obtained by writing:

U.S. DEPARTMENT OF COMMERCE
Patent and Trademark Office
Washington, D.C. 20231

Or by calling: (703) 557-INFO

This form is estimated to take 15 minutes to complete. Time will vary depending upon the needs of the individual case. Any comments on the amount of time you require to complete this form should be sent to the Office of Management and Organization, U.S. Patent and Trademark Office, U.S. Department of Commerce, Washington D.C., 20231, and to the Office of Information and Regulatory Affairs, Office of Management and Budget, Washington, D.C. 20503.

APPENDIX L

FEDERAL TRADEMARK REGISTRATION

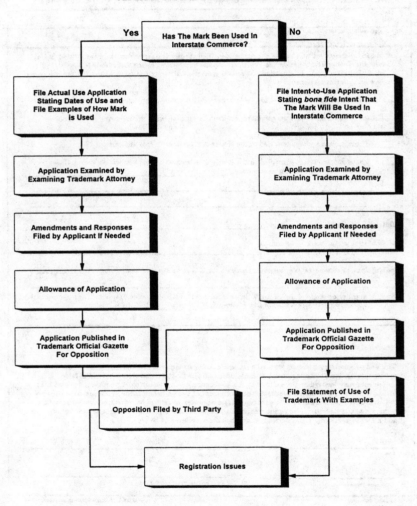

APPENDIX M

<table>
<tr><td colspan="2">

STATEMENT OF USE
UNDER 37 CFR 2.88, WITH
DECLARATION

</td><td>

MARK (identify the mark)

SERIAL NO

</td></tr>
</table>

TO THE ASSISTANT SECRETARY AND COMMISSIONER OF PATENTS AND TRADEMARKS:

APPLICANT NAME

NOTICE OF ALLOWANCE ISSUE DATE.

Applicant requests registration of the above-identified trademark/service mark in the United States Patent and Trademark Office on the Principal Register established by the Act of July 5, 1946 (15 U.S.C. 1051 et. seq., as amended). Three (3) specimens showing the mark as used in commerce are submitted with this statement.

☐ Check here only if a Request to Divide under 37 CFR 2.87 is being submitted with this Statement.

Applicant is using the mark in commerce on or in connection with the following goods/services: (Check One)

☐ Those goods/services identified in the Notice of Allowance in this application.

☐ Those goods/services identified in the Notice of Allowance in this application except: (Identify goods/services to be deleted from application) _____

_____

_____

Date of first use of mark anywhere: _____

Date of first use of mark in commerce
which the U.S. Congress may regulate: _____

Specify type of commerce: (e.g., interstate, between the U.S. and a specified foreign country) _____

_____

Specify manner or mode of use of mark on or in connection with the goods/services: (e.g., trademark is applied to labels, service mark is used in advertisements) _____

_____

The undersigned being hereby warned that willful false statements and the like so made are punishable by fine or imprisonment, or both, under 18 U.S.C. 1001, and that such willful false statements may jeopardize the validity of the application or any resulting registration, declares that he/she is properly authorized to execute this Statement of Use on behalf of the applicant; he/she believes the applicant to be the owner of the trademark/service mark sought to be registered; the trademark/service mark is now in use in commerce; and all statements made of his/her own knowledge are true and all statements made on information and belief are believed to be true.

Date	Signature
Telephone Number	Print or Type Name and Position

PTO Form 1580 (REV. 9-89)
OMB No. 0651-0023
Exp. 6-30-82

U.S. DEPARTMENT OF COMMERCE/Patent and Trademark Office

INSTRUCTIONS AND INFORMATION FOR APPLICANT

In an application based upon a bona fide intention to use a mark in commerce, applicant must use its mark in commerce before a registration will be issued. After use begins, the applicant must submit, along with evidence of use (specimens) and the prescribed fee(s), either:

> (1) an Amendment to Allege Use under 37 CFR 2.76, or
> (2) a Statement of Use under 37 CFR 2.88.

The difference between these two filings is the timing of the filing. Applicant may file an Amendment to Allege Use before approval of the mark for publication for opposition in the Official Gazette, or, if a final refusal has been issued, prior to the expiration of the six month response period. Otherwise, applicant must file a Statement of Use after the Office issues a Notice of Allowance. The Notice of Allowance will issue after the opposition period is completed if no successful opposition is filed. Neither Amendment to Allege Use or Statement of Use papers will be accepted by the Office during the period of time between approval of the mark for publication for opposition in the Official Gazette and the issuance of the Notice of Allowance.

Applicant may call (703) 557-5249 to determine whether the mark has been approved for publication for opposition in the Official Gazette.

Before filing an Amendment to Allege Use or a Statement of Use, applicant must use the mark in commerce on or in connection with all of the goods/services for which applicant will seek registration, unless applicant submits with the papers, a request to divide out from the application the goods or services to which the Amendment to Allege Use or Statement of Use pertains. (See: 37 CFR 2.87, Dividing an application)

Applicant must submit with an Amendment to Allege Use or a Statement of Use:

> (1) the appropriate fee of $100 per class of goods/services listed in the Amendment to Allege Use or the Statement of Use, and

> (2) three (3) specimens or facsimiles of the mark as used in commerce for each class of goods/services asserted (e.g., photograph of mark as it appears on goods, label containing mark which is placed on goods, or brochure or advertisement showing mark as used in connection with services).

Cautions/Notes concerning completion of this Statement of Use form:

> (1) The goods/services identified in the Statement of Use must be identical to the goods/services identified in the Notice of Allowance. Applicant may delete goods/services. Deleted goods/services may not be reinstated in the application at a later time.

> (2) Applicant may list dates of use for only one item in each class of goods/services identified in the Statement of Use. However, applicant must have used the mark in commerce on all the goods/services in the class. Applicant must identify the particular item to which the dates apply.

> (3) Only the following person may sign the verification of the Statement of Use, depending on the applicant's legal entity: (a) the individual applicant; (b) an officer of corporate applicant; (c) one general partner of partnership applicant; (d) all joint applicants.

This form is estimated to take 15 minutes to complete. Time will vary depending upon the needs of the individual case. Any comments on the amount of time you require to complete this form should be sent to the Office of Management and Organization, U.S. Patent and Trademark Office, U.S. Department of Commerce, Washington D.C., 20231, and to the Office of Information and Regulatory Affairs, Office of Management and Budget, Washington, D.C. 20503.

APPENDIX N

<table>
<tr><td rowspan="3">REQUEST FOR EXTENSION OF TIME
UNDER 37 CFR 2.89 TO FILE A STATEMENT
OF USE, WITH DECLARATION</td><td>MARK (Identify the mark)</td></tr>
<tr><td>SERIAL NO</td></tr>
</table>

TO THE ASSISTANT SECRETARY AND COMMISSIONER OF PATENTS AND TRADEMARKS:

APPLICANT NAME

NOTICE OF ALLOWANCE MAILING DATE:

Applicant requests a six-month extension of time to file the Statement of Use under 37 CFR 2.88 in this application.

☐ Check here if a Request to Divide under 37 CFR 2.87 is being submitted with this request.

Applicant has a continued bona fide intention to use the mark in commerce in connection with the following goods/services: (Check one below)

☐ Those goods/services identified in the Notice of Allowance in this application.

☐ Those goods/services identified in the Notice of Allowance in this application except: (Identify goods/services to be deleted from application) _____

_____

This is the _____ request for an Extension of Time following mailing of the Notice of Allowance.
(Specify first - 5th)
If this is not the first request for an Extension of Time, check one box below. If the first box is checked, explain the circumstance(s) of the non-use in the space provided:

☐ Applicant has not used the mark in commerce yet on all goods/services specified in the Notice of Allowance; however, applicant has made the following ongoing efforts to use the mark in commerce on or in connection with each of the goods/services specified above:

_____

_____
If additional space is needed, please attach a separate sheet to this form

☐ Applicant believes that it has made valid use of the mark in commerce, as evidenced by the Statement of Use submitted with this request; however, if the Statement of Use is found by the Patent and Trademark Office to be fatally defective, applicant will need additional time in which to file a new statement.

The undersigned being hereby warned that willful false statements and the like so made are punishable by fine or imprisonment, or both, under 18 U.S.C. 1001, and that such willful false statements may jeopardize the validity of the application or any resulting registration, declares that he/she is properly authorized to execute this Request for Extension of Time to File a Statement of Use on behalf of the applicant; he/she believes the applicant to be the owner of the trademark/service mark sought to be registered; and all statements made of his/her own knowledge are true and all statements made on information and belief are believed to be true.

Date _____   Signature _____

Telephone Number _____   Print or Type Name and Position _____

PTO Form 1581 (REV. 5-89)
OMB No. 0651-0023
Exp. 6-30-92

U.S. DEPARTMENT OF COMMERCE/Patent and Trademark Office

100

INSTRUCTIONS AND INFORMATION FOR APPLICANT

Applicant must file a Statement of Use within six months after the mailing of the Notice of Allowance in an application based upon a bona fide intention to use a mark in commerce, UNLESS, within that same period, applicant submits a request for a six-month extension of time to file the Statement of Use. The request **must**:

(1) be in writing,
(2) include applicant's verified statement of continued bona fide intention to use the mark in commerce,
(3) specify the goods/services to which the request pertains as they are identified in the Notice of Allowance, and
(4) include a fee of $100 for each class of goods/services.

Applicant may request four further six-month extensions of time. No extension may extend beyond 36 months from the issue date of the Notice of Allowance. Each request must be filed within the previously granted six-month extension period and must include, in addition to the above requirements, a showing of GOOD CAUSE. This good cause showing must include:

(1) applicant's statement that the mark has not been used in commerce yet on all the goods or services specified in the Notice of Allowance with which applicant has a continued bona fide intention to use the mark in commerce, **and**

(2) applicant's statement of ongoing efforts to make such use, which may include the following: (a) product or service research or development, (b) market research, (c) promotional activities, (d) steps to acquire distributors, (e) steps to obtain required governmental approval, or (f) similar specified activity .

Applicant may submit one additional six-month extension request during the existing period in which applicant files the Statement of Use, unless the granting of this request would extend beyond 36 months from the issue date of the Notice of Allowance. As a showing of good cause, applicant should state its belief that applicant has made valid use of the mark in commerce, as evidenced by the submitted Statement of Use, but that if the Statement is found by the PTO to be defective, applicant will need additional time in which to file a new statement of use.

Only the following person may sign the verification of the Request for Extension of Time, depending on the applicant's legal entity: (a) the individual applicant; (b) an officer of corporate applicant; (c) one general partner of partnership applicant; (d) all joint applicants.

APPENDIX O
STATES HAVING
TRADE SECRET STATUTES

Alabama	Maryland
Alaska	Minnesota
Arizona	Mississippi
Arkansas	Montana
California	Nevada
Colorado	New Hampshire
Connecticut	New Mexico
Delaware	North Carolina
District of Columbia	North Dakota
Florida	Oklahoma
Hawaii	Oregon
Idaho	Rhode Island
Illinois	South Dakota
Indiana	Texas
Iowa	Utah
Kansas	Virginia
Kentucky	Washington
Louisiana	West Virginia
Maine	Wisconsin

Appendix P
Confidential Disclosure Agreement

Subject Matter: _____

Date of Disclosure: _____

In consideration of the disclosure of Confidential Information relating to the above-identified subject matter made by _____ whose address is _____ (hereinafter "Discloser") to _____ whose address is _____ (hereinafter "Recipient") who desires to receive such information for evaluation purposes only, the Recipient hereby expressly agrees that any and all Confidential Information disclosed to Recipient by Discloser, its agents, employees or other persons acting in concert with or on behalf of Discloser, shall be maintained and treated as Confidential as if such Confidential Information was that of Recipient. Recipient further agrees that the disclosed Confidential Information shall not be used in any manner whatsoever, disclosed to others, copied or reproduced by the Recipient without first obtaining written permission from Discloser.

For purposes of this Confidential Disclosure Agreement, Confidential Information includes, but is not limited to, all information, whether embodied in tangible form or not, relating to all ideas, concepts, inventions, improvements, methods which may be embodied in documents, tangible things or any other form of information disclosed. The foregoing includes without limitation registered and unregistered copyrights, trademarks or service marks and trade names, patents pending or issued, which are disclosed, orally, in writing, or by electronic means by Discloser to Recipient.

_____
Recipient

_____
Firm Name

Appendix Q
Additional Information Sources

PATENTS

The Patent and Trademark Office strongly advises you to consult a registered patent attorney or agent before attempting to file an application. Names of patent attorneys and agents may be obtained from classified telephone directories in major cities, or from a directory published by the Government Printing Office.

For more information, the book <u>General Information Concerning Patents</u>, is available from the Superintendent of Documents, Government Printing Office, Washington, D.C. 20402. (doc.#003-004-626-9, price $2.00)

For specific questions write to the Public Service Center, Patent and Trademark Office, Washington, D.C. 20231, or call (703) 557-INFO.

TRADEMARKS

To receive a copy of the <u>Basic Facts About Trademarks</u> booklet, complete with model filing forms, write to the Superintendent of Documents, Government Printing Office, Washington, D.C. 20402 (doc. #003-004-00642-1, price $1.00). For further information write The Public Service Center, Patent and Trademark Office, Washington, D.C. 20231, or call (703) 557-INFO.

COPYRIGHTS

Information concerning copyrights may be obtained from the Library of Congress, Information Section, LM-455 Copyright Office, Washington, D.C. 20559, Telephone (202) 479-0700.

Copyright registration forms are available by requesting the appropriate form in writing at:

Copyright Office
LM 455
Library of Congress
Washington, D.C. 20559
(202) 707-9100

Rules for obtaining Patents, Trademarks and Copyrights are found in the Code of Federal Regulations, Title 37. Each year the Government Printing Office in Washington, D.C. publishes a new edition of the rules. This edition is published as of July 1 of each year. Be certain that you have the most recent set of rules available to you. The rules are updated by the U.S. Patent and Trademark Office and published weekly in the <u>Official Gazette</u> of the United States Patent and Trademark Office. Copies of the Code of Federal Regulations may be obtained by writing to:

Superintendent of Documents
Attn: New Orders
P.O. Box 371954
Pittsburgh, PA 15250-7954

Telephone orders with a credit card may be made by telephoning the order desk at the United States Government Printing Office at (202)783-3238.

Appendix R

Publications available for purchase from the Government Printing Office

PATENTS

General Information Concerning Patents, 1992
Commerce Dept., Patent and Trademark Office
1992: 43 p., 4 forms. revised ed.
003-004-00659-5 Each $2.25

Manual of Patent Examining Procedure
Commerce Dept., Patent and Trademark Office
Subscription $78.00

Index of Patents, 1991, Issued From the United States Patent
and Trademark Office, Pt. 2, Index to Subjects of Invention
Commerce Dept., Patent and Trademark Office 1992: 687 p.
Each $38.00

Index of Patents, 1991, Issued From the United States Patent
and Trademark Office, Pt. 1, List of Patentees Commerce Dept.,
Patent and Trademark Office 1991: 2 bks. (3946 p.)
Each $72.00

Index to the United States Patent Classification: 1991, Dec.
Commerce Dept., Patent and Trademark Office, Office of
Classification Support 1991: 255 p.
Each $13.00

Challenge of Technological Change
Congress, Office of Technology Assessment
1992: 236 p. OTA-TCT-527; Item 1070-M.
Each $11.00

Attorneys and Agents Registered to Practice Before the United
States Patent and Trademark Office, 1992 Each $26.00

Concordance: United States Patent Classification to International Patent Classification, 1990
Commerce Dept., Patent and Trademark Office, Administrator for Documentation 1990: 188 p. Item 254-A; Each $10.00

New Developments in Biotechnology, 5: Patenting Life
Congress, Office of Technology Assessment
1989: 201 p.; ill. OTA-BA-370. L.C. card 88-600596. Item 1070-M; Each $8.50.

Official Gazette of the United States Patent and Trademark Office Patents Commerce Dept., Patent and Trademark Office ISSN 0098-1133. Item 260; Subscription $516.00.

Manual of Classification of Patents
Commerce Dept., Patent and Trademark Office, Office of Documentation Planning and Support; Revised Dec. 1990
Subscription $82.00

TRADEMARKS

Basic Facts About Trademarks, 1992
Commerce Dept., Patent and Trademark Office
1992: 30 p.; ill. revised ed.
Item 254; Each $2.25

Code of Federal Regulations, Title 37, Patents, Trademarks, and Copyrights, Revised as of July 1, 1992
National Archives and Records Administration, Office of the Federal Register 1992: 530 p.
Each $17.00

Index of Trademarks Issued From the United States Patent and Trademark Office, 1991
Commerce Dept., Patent and Trademark Office 1992: 1219 p.
Item 256-C; Each $51.00

Patent and Trademark Office Notices
Commerce Dept., Patent and Trademark Office
703-035-00000-1; Item 260; Subscription $74.00.

Trademark Manual of Examining Procedure
Commerce Dept., Patent and Trademark Office
903-010-00000-2; Item 254-A; Subscription $19.00.

Official Gazette of the United States Patent and Trademark
Office: Trademarks
Commerce Dept., Patent and Trademark Office
703-034-00000-4; Item 260; $410.00

COPYRIGHTS

Copyright Law
Gorman, Robert A.
Administrative Office of United States Courts, Federal Judicial
Center, Editorial Office 1991: 164 p.
Each $5.00

Copyright Law of the United States of America
Library of Congress, Copyright Office
1991: 132 p.
Item 802-A; Each $3.75

Copyright and Home Copying: Technology Challenges the Law
Congress, Office of Technology Assessment 1989: 301 p.; ill.
OTA-CIT-422. L.C. card 89-600714. Item 1070-M; Each $13.00

Copyright in Works of Architecture: A Report of the Register of
Copyrights
Library of Congress, Copyright Office 1989: 361 p.; ill. ISBN 0-
8444-0653-8. L.C.card 89-600213; Each $18.00

Technological Alterations to Motion Pictures and Other Audiovisual Works: Implications for Creators, Copyright Owners,
and Consumers, A Report.
Library of Congress, Register of Copyrights 1989: 3 bks. (1064
pages)
ISBN 0-8444-0642-2. L.C. card 89-600068. Item 803; Set $36.00

Index

A

Agents, 13, 53
Alabama, 115
Alaska, 115
Annuals, 51 (see Copyright)
Architectural blueprints, 46 (see Copyright)
Arizona, 34, 115
Arkansas, 115
Arlington, Virginia, 13-14
Art Unit, 24 (see also Patent, evaluation of)
Attorney, 13, 28, 32, 52, 54
"Attorneys and Agents Registered to Practice Before the United States Patent and Trademark Office," 121
Audiovisual works, 44-45, 51 (see Copyright)
Authors, 7, 44-45, 53

B

"Basic Facts About Trademarks," 119, 122
Bona fide intention to use, 6 (See Registered trademark)
Books, 4, 42, 45, 51 (see Copyright)
Brand name, 31 (see Service Mark)
Breach of contract claim, 57 (see Trade secrets)

C

California, 34, 115
CD-ROMs, 7 (see Copyright)
Certificate of registration, 54 (see Copyright)

Certification mark, 35 (see also Trademark)
"Challenge of Technological Change," 121
Chemical formulations, 4 (see Patents)
Claim for Small Entity Status, 92
Co-author, 7 (see Author)
Coca-Cola, 8
"Code of Federal Regulations," 122
Collective mark, 35 (see also Trademark)
Colorado, 115
Common law rights, 5-6, 31-34
Common property, 46
Composition of matter, 9, 10, 11 (see Patents, Utility patents)
Compulsory license, 44 (see Copyright)
Computer programs, 4, 42, 46 (see Copyright)
"Concordance: United States Patent Classification to International Patent Classification," 122
Confidential Disclosure Agreement (sample), 117
Confidential information, 8, 56 (see Trade secrets)
Confidentiality agreements, 57 (see Trade secrets)
Congress, 1
Connecticut, 115
Contributory infringer, 28
Copyright
    amending application, 52

eligibility for, 2
enforcing, 55
fees, 3, 52, 54
filing for renewal of term, 50, 52
protection under law, 1-2, 7,
    42-46
registering work, 42, 47-48,
    50-54
terms for anonymous
    works, 48-50
term for authors, 43, 49
term for corporations, 43, 49
term for joint work, 49
terms for works published before
    1978, 50
types of work covered, 4, 7, 43-44
use of, 3, 7-8
work not eligible for, 46
"Copyright and Home Copying,"
    123
Copyright claimant, 53
"Copyright in works of
    architecture," 123
"Copyright Law," 123
"Copyright Law of the United
    States of America," 123
Copyright notice, 42, 47-49
Copyright owner, 42, 53
Copyright symbol, 42, 49
Copy registration application forms
    Form CA, 52
    Form GR/CP, 52
    Form PA, 51
    Form RE, 52
    Form SE, 51
    Form SR, 52
    Form TX, 51
    Form VA, 52

D
Dance choreography, 7, 44-45, 51
    (see Copyright)

Declaration by owner
    patent application, 23, 84
    registered trademark, 38
Delaware, 115
Design patents,
    definition, 9
    term, 10
Device patents, 9 (see Utility
    patents)
Doctrine of Equivalents, 28 (see
    also Infringement, patents)
Doctrine of "fair use" 44 (see
    Copyright, protection)

E
Employer, 44 (see Copyright,
    protection)
Employment agreement, 57 (see
    Trade secrets)
Entrepreneurs, 1 (see also
    Inventors)
Examining Trademark Attorney,
    38-39
Extension Request form, 40 (see
    Registered Trademark)

F
Florida, 115
Florida Citrus Grower's
    Association, 35

G
"General Information Concerning
    Patents," 119, 121
Government Printing Office,
    119-123

H
Hawaii, 115
Holograms, 7 (see Copyright)

I
Idaho, 115
Ideas, 1-2

Illinois, 115
Illustrations, 7 (see Copyright)
Improvements, 9-10 (see Patents, Utility patent)
Independent Contractors, 42 (see also Copyright, protection)
"Index of Patents," 121
"Index of Trademarks Issued from the United States Patent and Trademark Office," 122
"Index to United States Patent Classification," 15, 121 (see also Patent search)
Indiana, 115
Information Disclosure Citation form, 96
Infringement
  copyright, 50-51
  patents, 19, 27-29
  trademark, 33
Intangible property, 4 (see also Intellectual property)
Intellectual property
  definition, 4
  law, 1, 4
  rights, 1-2, 4-8, 56
  types, 4
Intent-to-use mark, 37 (see Registered Trademark)
International Classification (of goods and services), 35, 38
Interstate commerce, 34, 40 (see Registered trademark)
Invention priority date, 23 (see also Patent, filing an application)
Inventions, 1-2, 9, 15, 20, 22-27
Inventors, 1, 9, 13, 20-25
Iowa, 115

J
Joint works, 45 (see Copyright)
Journals, 51

K
Kansas, 115
Kentucky, 115
Kleenex, 30 (see also Trademark)

L
Library of Congress, 48, 119-120
Literal patent infringement, 28 (see also Infringement, patents)
Logo, 4, 31 (see Trademarks, Service Marks)
Louisiana, 115
Lyrics, 4 (see Copyright)

M
Machines, 4, 9, 10, 11 (see Patents, Utility patents)
Magazine, 7, 45, 51 (see Copyright)
Maine, 115
"Manual of Classification of Patents," 122
"Manual of Patent Examining Procedures," 121
Manufactured articles, 9 (see Design patents)
Manufacturing processes, 4, 9, 10, 11 (see Patents, Utility patent)
Mark, 1, 30 (see Trademark, Service Mark)
Market area, 6, 32
Marketing, 4
Markings, 1 (see Trademark, Service Mark)
Maryland, 115
Mask works, 8 (see Copyright)
Minnesota, 115
Mississippi, 115
Montana, 115
Movie scripts, 7, 44-45, 51 (see Copyright)

Multi-class application, 38 (see Registered Trademark)
Music, 4, 7, 43, 45, 51 (see Copyright)

N
Names, 4, (see Trademarks, Service Marks)
Nevada, 115
"New Developments in Biotechnology," 122
New Hampshire, 115
New Mexico, 115
Newsletter, 51
Newspaper, 7, 45, 51 (see Copyright)
Newsweek, 7
Non-disclosure contract, 56 (see Trade secrets)
Non-obviousness requirement, 12-13, 16-19, 26-27 (see Patents, requirements for patentability)
Non-patent references, 15, 16 (see also Patent search)
North Carolina, 115
North Dakota, 115
Notice of Allowance, 40 (see Registered trademark)
Novelty requirement, 12-13, 16, 21, 26-27 (see Patents, requirements for patentability)

O
Office Action
  patent, 26
  registered trademark, 39
"Official Gazette of the United States Patent and Trademark Office," 122, 123
Oklahoma, 115
Oregon, 115

Original works of authorship, 7, 42, 44-45 (see Copyright)

P
Paintings, 7, 45 (see Copyright)
Pantomimes, 44-45, 51 (see Copyright)
Pat. No., 1 (see also Patents)
Patent
  amending an application, 22, 26
  appeal of rejected claim, 26
  classification of, 15
  definition, 9
  eligibility, 2
  enforcement of, 9, 13, 26-27
  evaluation of, 14-17, 24-27
  fees, 3, 24, 26, 86-87
  filing application for, 13, 19-23, 84
  foreign, 5, 21
  information disclosure citation form, 96
  prosecution flow chart, 98
  process flow chart, 100
  protection under law, 1-2, 4-5, 20, 26-29
  public disclosure, 20-23, 24-25
  requirements for patentability, 5, 10-12, 25, 27
  registered, 2
  rights of owner, 1, 5, 9
  sample, 60-73, 76-77
  term of, 9-10, 22, 25
  types of, 9-10
  types of subject matter covered, 4-5, 10-12
Patent agent, 14, 20-21, 119
Patent and Trademark Depository Libraries, 13-14, 39, 80-82
"Patent and Trademark Office Notices," 122
Patent application transmittal letter, 24, 94

Patent attorney, 14, 20-21, 119

Patent claim, 22, 25-27 (see Patent, filing an application)

Patent Depository Library, 13-14

Patent Examiner, 24-27

Patent owner, 5, 28 (see also Inventor)

Patent pending, 1, 27

Patent prosecution (flowcharts), 98, 100

Patent references, 15, 16 (see Patent search)

Patent search, 13-16, 19-20, 25

Patent searchers, 14

Patentee, 9 (see Inventor)

Performing art, 7 (see Copyright)

Periodicals, 51 (see Copyright)

Petition for Small Entity Status, 23, 92

Phonograph record, 7 (see Copyright)

Photographs, 7, 45, 52 (see Copyright)

Pictures, 4, 44-45, 52 (see Copyright)

Plants (asexually reproduced), 10

Plant patents definition, 10

Poems, 7, 45 (see Copyright)

Power of Attorney Assignment Agreement, 23

Presumptive validity, 50 (see Copyright, registering for)

Principal Register, 35 (see Registered trademark, types of)

Prior art, 15-16, 26-27 (see also Patent search)

Process patents, 9 (see Utility patents)

Proprietary information, 56 (see Trade secrets)

Proprietary rights agreement, 57 (see Trade secrets)

Prototype, 20 (see also Invention)

Public record, 50 (see Copyright, registering for)

Publication, 47-48 (see Copyright)

R

Registered trademarks
  actual use application, 6, 36-41
  advantages of registration, 31
  amending the application, 39
  commercial use of, 39
  enforcing rights, 35, 41
  federal registration system, 6, 33-35, 106
  fees, 38
  filing an application, 33, 36-38, 102-103
  intent-to-use application, 6, 36-40
  penalty of non-use of mark, 41
  protection under law, 2, 6, 30-35, 38
  search, 30, 32, 38-39
  state registration system, 33-34
  term, 31, 41
  types of registration, 35-38
Request for Extension of Time (to file Statement of Use form) (sample form, 112-113
Rhode Island, 115
Rules of Practice and Ethics, 13

S

Scottsdale, Arizona, 34
Sculpture, 7, 44-45, 52 (see Copyright)
Secretary of State, 33
Serial works, 51
Service Marks
  types of marks, 31
  types of property covered, 4
Slogans, 5

Small entity, 24
Small Entity Declaration, 24, 92
Sound recordings, 7, 46, 52 (see Copyright)
South Dakota, 115
Statement of Use form, 40, 108-109 (see Registered Trademark)
Statutory bar, 20, 23 (see Patent, public disclosure)
Supplemental Register, 35-36 (see Registered Trademark, types of)
Symbols, 1, 30-31 (see also Trademark, Service Mark, Copyright)

T

Tangible property, 4, 45 (see also Intellectual property)
"Technological Alterations to Motion Pictures and Other Audiovisual Works," 123
Temporary personnel, 42 (see also Copyright, protection)
Texas, 115
Textual works, 7, 45 (see Copyright)
Theatrical performances, 7, 45, 51 (see Copyright)
Theatrical scripts, 7, 45, 51 (see Copyright)
Time Magazine, 7
Trade dress, (see Trademark)
Trademark
  eligibility, 2
  fees, 3, 88-89
  protection under law, 1-2, 5-7, 30-33
  registering, 33-41
  types of marks, 31
  types of property covered, 4
  use of, 3, 30-31

"Trademark Manual of Examining Procedure," 123
Trade name, 5 (see Trademark)
Trademark Official Gazette, 39, 120
Trademark owner, 34
Trade secrets,
  as replacement for patent, 57
  enforcing confidentiality agreements, 57-58
  licensing of trade secrets, 58
  protection under law, 4-5, 8, 56-57
  sample confidential disclosure agreement, 117
  states that have statutes, 115
  term of, 57
Trademark/Service Mark Application (sample form), 102-103
Trademark Trial and Appeal Board, 40

U

UL mark, 35
Underwriter's Laboratories, 35
Uniform Trade Secrets Act, 8, 56
Unpublished works, 48-49 (see Copyright)
U.S. Code
  Title 15, 7
  Title 17, 7
  Title 35, 5
  Title 35, Section 101, 10
  Title 35, Section 103, 12
  Title 35, Section 154, 9
  Title 37, 119
U.S. Constitution, 1
U.S. Copyright Act, 43, 47, 55
U.S. Copyright Office, 2, 42, 47-48, 50, 54
U.S. District Court, 28, 55

U.S. Patent and Trademark Office
   (PTO), 2, 10, 12-14, 21, 23, 25,
   27, 31-33, 35-36, 38-41, 119-120
Use patents, 9 (see Utility patent)
Utah, 115
Utility patent
   definition, 9
   term of, 10
Utility requirement, 12-13, 27 (see
   Patents, requirements for
      patentability)

V
Videotaped recordings, 7 (see
   Copyright)
Virginia, 115
Visual art, 7 (see Copyright)

W
Washington, 115
Washington, D.C., 14, 42, 115, 119
West Virginia, 115
Wisconsin, 115
Work made for hire, 44-45, 49

X
Xerox, 30 (see Trademark)

Y
Yellow pages, 32